First World War
and Army of Occupation
War Diary
France, Belgium and Germany

16 DIVISION
49 Infantry Brigade
Royal Inniskilling Fusiliers
7th Battalion
1 February 1916 - 31 August 1917

WO95/1977/2

The Naval & Military Press Ltd
www.nmarchive.com
Published in association with The National Archives

Published by

The Naval & Military Press Ltd

Unit 10 Ridgewood Industrial Park,

Uckfield, East Sussex,

TN22 5QE England

Tel: +44 (0) 1825 749494

www.naval-military-press.com

www.nmarchive.com

This diary has been reprinted in facsimile from the original. Any imperfections are inevitably reproduced and the quality may fall short of modern type and cartographic standards.

© Crown Copyright
Images reproduced by permission of The National Archives, London, England, 2015.

Contents

Document type	Place/Title	Date From	Date To
Heading	1977/2 7 Battalion Royal Iniskilling Fusiliers Feb 1916-Aug 1917		
Heading	16th Division 49th Infy Bde 7th Bn Roy Innis Fus. Feb 1916-Aug 1917 from UK with 8 Bn Aug 1917		
War Diary	Bordon	01/02/1916	19/02/1916
War Diary	Nedon	20/02/1916	25/02/1916
War Diary	L'Eclenie	26/02/1916	01/03/1916
War Diary	Philosophe	02/03/1916	20/03/1916
War Diary	Vaudricourt	21/03/1916	21/03/1916
War Diary	Canchy A-La-Tour	22/03/1916	26/03/1916
War Diary	Noeux Les Mines.	27/03/1916	01/04/1916
War Diary	In The Field	01/04/1916	06/04/1916
War Diary	Philosophe	07/04/1916	09/04/1916
War Diary	In The Field	10/04/1916	12/04/1916
War Diary	Mazingarbe	13/04/1916	20/04/1916
War Diary	Philosophe West	21/04/1916	24/04/1916
War Diary	In The Field	25/04/1916	26/04/1916
War Diary	Firingline Hulluck Right Sub Section	27/04/1916	29/04/1916
War Diary	Hulluck Sector	29/04/1916	29/04/1916
War Diary	Hulluck	29/04/1916	29/04/1916
War Diary	Philosophe	30/04/1916	06/05/1916
War Diary	Noeux Les Mines	07/05/1916	17/05/1916
War Diary	In The Field	18/05/1916	22/05/1916
War Diary	Mazingarbe	01/05/1916	25/05/1916
War Diary	In The Field	23/05/1916	30/05/1916
War Diary	In The Field	26/05/1916	31/05/1916
Heading	War Diary of 7th (S) Batt. Royal Inniskilling Fusiliers From 1st June 1916 to 30th June 1916 (Volume) 7 Inniskilling Vol 5 June		
War Diary	Philosophe	01/06/1916	02/06/1916
War Diary	Noeux Les Mines	03/06/1916	10/06/1916
War Diary	In The Field	11/06/1916	26/06/1916
War Diary	Mazingarbe	27/06/1916	30/06/1916
Heading	War Diary 7th (S) Battn Royal Inniskilling Fus 1st. July to 31st July 1916 Volume No. 6		
War Diary	Mazingarbe	01/07/1916	08/07/1916
War Diary	In The Field	09/07/1916	20/07/1916
War Diary	Trenches	22/07/1916	22/07/1916
War Diary	Noeux	26/07/1916	31/07/1916
Miscellaneous	Operations		
Miscellaneous	Received from OC 8th R. Innis Fus	16/07/1916	16/07/1916
War Diary	Philosophe	16/07/1916	16/07/1916
War Diary	Noeux-Les Mines	25/07/1916	29/07/1916
Heading	War Diary. 7th Royal Inniskilling Fusiliers Month Of August, 1916 Volume 7		
War Diary	Philosophe W	01/08/1916	04/08/1916
War Diary	Left Sub Sect	05/08/1916	05/08/1916
War Diary	14 Bis Section	06/08/1916	08/08/1916
War Diary	10th AV:	09/08/1916	16/08/1916
War Diary	Mazingarbe	17/08/1916	29/08/1916

War Diary	Lapugnoy	26/08/1916	28/08/1916
War Diary	Vaux. Sur Somme	29/08/1916	30/08/1916
War Diary	Gibraltar Near Bray Sur Somme	31/08/1916	31/08/1916
Heading	War Diary 7th Royal Inniskilling Fusiliers For Month Of September, 1916 Volume 8		
War Diary	Gibraltar Camp	01/09/1916	02/09/1916
War Diary	Citadel	03/09/1916	03/09/1916
War Diary	Nr Baay-Sur-Somme Billon Farm	03/09/1916	03/09/1916
War Diary	Leuze Wood	04/09/1916	08/09/1916
War Diary	Guillemont	08/09/1916	11/09/1916
War Diary	Sailly Le Sec.	18/09/1916	18/09/1916
War Diary	Bailleul	20/09/1916	20/09/1916
War Diary	Berthem	23/09/1916	23/09/1916
War Diary	Kemmel Shelters	27/09/1916	27/09/1916
Miscellaneous	7th (S) Bn. R. Inniskilling Fusiliers.	10/09/1916	10/09/1916
Heading	War Diary Month Of October, 1916 Volume 9 7th Royal Inniskilling Fusiliers.		
War Diary	Kemmel Shelters	03/10/1916	17/10/1916
War Diary	Locre	21/10/1916	29/10/1916
Heading	War Diary. For Month Of November, 1916 Volume 10 7th R. Inniskilling Fusiliers		
War Diary	Locre	01/11/1916	30/11/1916
Operation(al) Order(s)	8th. R. Innis. Fus. Operation Order No 48	30/07/1916	30/07/1916
Heading	War Diary For Month Of December, 1916 Volume 11 7th R. Inniskilling Fusiliers.		
War Diary	Locre	06/12/1916	30/12/1916
War Diary	Kemmel Shelters	31/12/1916	01/01/1917
War Diary	Trenches	05/01/1917	08/01/1917
War Diary	Locre	11/01/1917	11/01/1917
War Diary	Trenches	12/01/1917	20/01/1917
War Diary	Front Line	01/01/1917	05/01/1917
War Diary	Kemmel Shelters	05/01/1917	11/01/1917
War Diary	Front Line	11/01/1917	30/01/1917
Heading	War Diary For Month Of February, 1917 Volume 13 Unit. 7th Btn R. Inniskilling Fus		
War Diary	Kemmel Shelters	01/02/1917	04/02/1917
War Diary	Trenches	06/02/1917	08/02/1917
War Diary	Derry Huts	10/02/1917	15/02/1917
War Diary	Locre	14/02/1917	17/02/1917
War Diary	Trenches	22/02/1917	26/02/1917
War Diary	In The Trenches	26/02/1917	26/02/1917
War Diary	In Brigade Reserve	27/02/1917	28/02/1917
Heading	War Diary For Month Of March, 1917. Volume 14 Unit. 7th Btn R. Inniskilling Fus.		
War Diary	Derry Huts	01/03/1917	02/03/1917
War Diary	Curragh Camp	03/03/1917	19/03/1917
War Diary	Butterfly Farm	20/03/1917	23/03/1917
War Diary	Front Line Trenches Vierstraat Sector	23/03/1917	25/03/1917
War Diary	In The Trenches	25/03/1917	26/03/1917
War Diary	In Bde Support	29/03/1917	31/03/1917
Heading	War Diary For Month Of April, 1917 Volume 15 Unit. 7th R. Inniskilling Fus.		
War Diary	Rossignol House	01/04/1917	01/04/1917
War Diary	Clare Camp	02/04/1917	07/04/1917
War Diary	Birr Barracks	08/04/1917	13/04/1917
War Diary	On The March	13/04/1917	15/04/1917

War Diary	Zouafques	16/04/1917	28/04/1917
War Diary	On The March	28/04/1917	30/04/1917
Heading	War Diary Volume. 16 For Month Of May, 1917 Unit. 7th Royal Inniskilling Fusrs		
War Diary	Murrumbridgee Camp	01/05/1917	01/05/1917
War Diary	On the Reninghelst La Clytte Road	02/05/1917	05/05/1917
War Diary	Diependaal Right Sub Section.	06/05/1917	09/05/1917
War Diary	De Zon Camp on La-Clytte Locre Rd	10/05/1917	10/05/1917
War Diary	Support Post in Vierstraat Sector	10/05/1917	11/05/1917
War Diary	Support Vierstraat Section	12/05/1917	14/05/1917
War Diary	Front Line	15/05/1917	18/05/1917
War Diary	Birr Barracks	18/05/1917	31/05/1917
Heading	War Diary. For Month Of June, 1917 Volume 17 Unit. 7th Battn Royal Inniskilling Fus.		
War Diary	Birr Barracks	01/06/1917	02/06/1917
War Diary	Butterfly Farm	03/06/1917	05/06/1917
War Diary	In The Line	05/06/1917	12/06/1917
War Diary	Merris	13/06/1917	14/06/1917
War Diary	Merris (Sheet France 36A. E26 F2C 3/1/2.7)	14/06/1917	14/06/1917
War Diary	Merris	14/06/1917	16/06/1917
War Diary	Merris Clare Camp (Sheet 28. M33a65.95)	17/06/1917	17/06/1917
War Diary	Clare Camp	18/06/1917	18/06/1917
War Diary	Merris Sheet 36A France F2b 3 1/2.7		
War Diary	Merris	18/06/1917	20/06/1917
War Diary	Eecke Area Sheet 27 S.E. B Series	21/06/1917	21/06/1917
War Diary	Eecke Area	22/06/1917	22/06/1917
War Diary	Broxelle Area Sheet 27 2d.2	23/06/1917	23/06/1917
War Diary	Buysscheure Farm Sheet 27 Ed 2 M5.C.8.4	23/06/1917	25/06/1917
War Diary	Buysscheure Farm	25/06/1917	29/06/1917
War Diary	Zudausques	30/06/1917	30/06/1917
Heading	War Diary For Month Of July, 1917 Volume 18 Unit. 8th R. Inniskilling Fuslrs		
War Diary	Zudausques Sheet 27A. SE W 2 and 3	01/07/1917	05/07/1917
War Diary	Tatinghem	05/07/1917	07/07/1917
War Diary	On The March	08/07/1917	09/07/1917
War Diary	Winnezeele Sheet 27NE J11a 95.4	09/07/1917	25/07/1917
War Diary	Watou L.8.C.9.5. Sheet 27 Ed.2	26/07/1917	26/07/1917
War Diary	Watou L.8C.9.5	26/07/1917	29/07/1917
War Diary	Watou Area L8C 9.5 Sheet 27Ed 2	30/07/1917	30/07/1917
War Diary	On The March	30/07/1917	30/07/1917
War Diary	'B' Camp G6d4.4 Sheet 28 N.W. Ed 5A	31/07/1917	31/07/1917
War Diary	On The March Camp H10 C Sheet 28 N.W. Ed5	31/07/1917	06/08/1917
War Diary	S.Q. Fm Ypres	07/08/1917	11/08/1917
War Diary	Brandhoek Area Toronto Camp.	12/08/1917	14/08/1917
War Diary	Square Farm. E by N of Ypres.	15/08/1917	16/08/1917
War Diary	O.B. Front Line.	16/08/1917	22/08/1917
War Diary	Achiet-Le-Petit.	23/08/1917	26/08/1917
War Diary	Ervilliers	28/08/1917	30/08/1917
War Diary	Ervilliers No 5 Camp	31/08/1917	31/08/1917

1977/2

7 Battalion Royal Inniskilling Fusiliers

Feb 1916 – Aug 1917.

16TH DIVISION
49TH INFY BDE

7TH BN ROY INNIS FUS.

FEB 1916 - AUG 1917

from UK

Amalgamated with 8BN
Aug 1917

WAR DIARY or INTELLIGENCE SUMMARY.

Febr 6 7th R Inniskilling Fus 2nd
May 1916

Place	Date	Hour	Summary of Events and Information	Remarks and references to Appendices
BORDON	1/2/16	12 noon	Orders received to mobilize for service overseas	A.e T
"	2/2/16		Mobilization proceeding	A.e T
"	13/4/16		Major H.N. Young R. Inniskilling Fusiliers assumed command of the B.tn with the rank. Rank of Lieut. Col, one Tomp. Lt. Col. M.J Hughes (Captain R.F.O) Mobilization proceeding	a.e T
"	14		"	a.e T
"	15		Battalion entrains at BORDON in three sections, distribution	a.e T
"	16		Southampton	a.e T
"	17		Sailed from Southampton at 5 PM for HAVRE on the S.S Mona Queen. 1st Transport under Lieut H.E Reid. Sailing on another boat	a.e T
"	18		Arrived HAVRE about 1.30 AM disembarked 7 AM marched up to No 1 Rest Camp (Days). Drew Gerrisht by the Transport 6 B.n via Dublin from North B.n Lighting 9 PM	a.e T

WAR DIARY or INTELLIGENCE SUMMARY

Army Form C. 2118.

Place	Date	Hour	Summary of Events and Information	Remarks and references to Appendices
	1916 19 4.5.		Detrained at BERGUETTE 6 p.m. & marched to NEDON. Officers: Lt W. H. Young, Capt. Pratt, Lt. Taggart, Lt. & Q.M. W. Reid, Sig. Off.; Lt. G. M.C Walker, M/g Off., Lieut D. McMahon, Transport Off., 2/Lieut H. F. Reid. A Coy Capt V. H. Parr, Capt Evan Collis, Lieut T. O'Connor, Lieut E. G. Allcorn, Lieut A. L's Bradlow (Suiting 7H), 2/Lt J. Cotter, 2/Lt H. W. Ruddock. B Coy Capt. J. Rey, Lt E. J. McCormack, Lt S. M. Foster, 2/Lt H. G. C. Trim Yla, 2/Lt Carroll. C Coy Maj: H. D. Reid (Lak Lt. IA), Capt J. J. L. Gibson, 2/Lt H. B. Mitchell, 2/Lt M. J. Doy, 2/Lt A. LePeuvre, 2/Lt H. J. Kenny. D Coy Capt. T. H. S. Trainor, Lt R. M. Murray, 2/Lt G. L. Henderson, 2/Lt F. A. Milligan, 2/Lt R. T. Sutton (Bombing 7H), 2/Lt H. P. McKenna, 2/Lt J. Cunningham. Attached Lieut G. A. Alley R.A.M.C.	O.E.T
NEDON	20. 21. 22. 23.	10 A.M	O.R. 995. Maj. R. Rose White aptd for duty (2nd in command) Inspected by Maj. Gen. Hickie, G/S com 16 Div; Maj R. Rose White. Drilling. Musketry. General Smartening up.	O.E.T
L'Etoune	26		Marched to Villers ou Billion on to W. J. BETHUNE	O.E.T

WAR DIARY
INTELLIGENCE SUMMARY
(Erase heading not required.)

Army Form C. 2118.

Place	Date	Hour	Summary of Events and Information	Remarks and references to Appendices
L'ÉTHUNE	26, 27, 28, 29	—	Lieut. E.J. McCormick attached to the 1/6 D.L.I. & Lieut for the Purpose of running the O/c Trenching.	a.c.T
	Apr 1			
PHILOSOPHE	2		Marched to PHILOSOPHE. In attachment to the 4 B 5 7 n J. B C e	a.c.T
	3	6 P.M.	Evening 3/4 C Coys attached H.Qrs of J Hr 4 B 5 7 n J. B C e arrived in to the trenches. A C to 10 15 B C i R 17 hrs B C to 10 12 H 4 1 C C to H 8 K 5 B i D C to H 7 K 5 B i T renches Loose unmistakably Noticeable. Snow R 5 7 ich Truth D C to H 7 K 5 B. T renches Loose unmistakably Noticeable. Snow R 5 7 ich Truth	
			Level, T.O 27 Lieut. at 2/L M.J Daly Struck Off the Strength of the B n and attached to B d e T rench Mortar Officers. 49 15 Tn J. B n order N° 77. D/3/3/16.	a.c.T
	4		Weather Serious R 5 7 L C t Shrewins. Trench 35° Day 25° 30° midnight Frost	
	5		N° 13419 Sgt W. J. M M 27.07 7 and D C to killed by Trench Whizt in trenches	a.c.T
	6		N° 2.4033 Pte G. McCauley "A" " (Self inflicted wounds) Weather Snow & Sleet 6 he ours. T emp 35° by day. 25-30 by night. Frost at night. 2.69 20 Pte R. Cellington "C" Coy died of wounds received in action 6/3/16.	

Army Form C. 2118.

WAR DIARY
or
INTELLIGENCE SUMMARY.
(Erase heading not required.)

Instructions regarding War Diaries and Intelligence Summaries are contained in F.S. Regs., Part II and the Staff Manual respectively. Title pages will be prepared in manuscript.

Place	Date	Hour	Summary of Events and Information	Remarks and references to Appendices
PHILOSOPHE	7			
"	8			
"	9		No.16511 Sgt T.W. McMurray 'A' Coy died of wounds	Q & T
"	10		No.24176 Pte J Jennings 'D' Coy; no 27030 Pte P Gallagher; No 22732 Pte Miller and No 13746 Pte M Morgan A Coy died of wounds received in action	Q & T
"	11			
"	12			
"	13		No.23035 Pte T Johnston killed in action 13/3/16	Q & T
"	14		Battalion returned from trenches after receiving instruction by Engineers and marched	Q & T
"	15		to PHILOSOPHE	
"	16		ST. PATRICK'S DAY. The battalion moved from PHILOSOPHE to the trenches at 5.30 p.m.	Q & T
"	17		to take over a sector of the line as a battalion	
"	18		2/Lieut. F J Kennymeevicated to England was struck off the strength, CAPT R S Kerr 'B' Coy reported for duty from England and was attached to 'C' Coy for instruction, Capt L & R Braddell reported for duty and posted to 'D' Coy as 2nd in command.	Q & T
"	19/20		Battalion relieved in trenches by 11th A.S.H. & returned to PHILOSOPHE	Q & T
"	20.		Battalion marched to VAUDRICOURT.	
VAUDRICOURT.	21.		Bn marched to CAUCHY-A-LA-TOUR.	Q & T

7th R. Inniskilling Fus
7th Inniskillings
Page 5 Vol 3
XVI
Army Form C. 2118.

WAR DIARY
or
INTELLIGENCE SUMMARY.
(Erase heading not required.)

Place	Date	Hour	Summary of Events and Information	Remarks and references to Appendices
Sailly-La-Bourse	22.3 to 26.3		2nd in Command Capt KERR took over command of 'B' Coy from Capt Ritty	
NOEUX LES MINES	27th		B's marched to LABUISNOY (5 miles) and entrained from there at 8-30 a.m.	
	28th March		Bn NOEUX-LES-MINES, at which place it arrived at 9-20 a.m.	
	to 1st April		Battalion billeted in NOEUX LES MINES. March 31st Lieut Col T.N. Young proceeded to ENGLAND on sick leave. Major G. F. BROOKE 6th CONNAUGHT RANGERS took over Company command of the Battalion during the absence of Lieut-Col Young.	
2nd in field	1st April		Battalion took over the LEFT of PUITS 14 BIS SECTOR, extending from CHALK PIT ALLEY on the right to POSEN ALLEY on the left 'A' 'B' and 'C' Coys in the firing line and 'D' Coy in SUPPORT RESERVE.	
"	2nd April to 6 April		Battalion held front line from 1st to night of 6/7 April 1916. C.S.M. Taylor 'A' Coy killed in action on 5th April. On the afternoon of 6th APRIL, the portion of the line held by 'B' Coy was heavily shelled from 1-5 p.m. to 2-45 p.m.; casualties were nil. Battalion relieved on night 6/7 APRIL by C.S.M. MEIRION 'B' Coy wounded on 6 April 1916. by 9th R. INNISKILLING FUSILIERS.	
PHILOSOPHE 7th APRIL	7th to 9th APRIL		Battalion arrived in PHILOSOPHE from the trenches at 4 a.m. Battalion billeted in PHILOSOPHE as battalion in BRIGADE RESERVE. On 9th night 9th April the Battalion relieved the 9th R IRISH FUS. in TENTH AVENUE as Battalion in SUPPORT.	
in the field	10th APRIL		Battalion in TENTH AVENUE. Deputations as follows:- 'A' Coy in SUN ALLEY, 'B' Coy two platoons in NORTHERN SAP, REDOUBT and 2 Platoons in 65 METRE POINT REDOUBT. 'C' and 'D' Coys in TENTH AVENUE.	
	11th APRIL		Lieut Col T.N. Young took over command of the Battalion on his return from ENGLAND.	

WAR DIARY
or
INTELLIGENCE SUMMARY.

Army Form C. 2118.

No 8

7th R. INNISKILLING

Place	Date	Hour	Summary of Events and Information	Remarks and references to Appendices
In the field	APRIL 12th		Battalion relieved on night 12/13th APRIL by the 8th MUNSTER FUSILIERS, and arrived in billets at MAZINGARBE at 9 p.m.	
MAZINGARBE	April 13th to 20th		Battalion in rest. 'B' coy inspected by G.O.C. 49th INF BDE on the 14th APRIL, and complimented for their heavy and arduous duties on the afternoon of the 8th APRIL. Certificates of merit & money were distributed by Brigadier General R. LEVESON-GOWER, 49th INF BDE to the following officers N.C.O. and men - CAPTS. R.E. KERR and RITTY. LIEUT. EN FLOOR. 2/LIEUT A.E.C. TRIMBLE. 25968 SERGT BRENNAN and 22505 PTE BROWN. On the 18th APRIL 'B' coy marched to NOEUX LES MINES when it was inspected by GENERAL SIR CHARLES MUNRO. K.C.B. LIEUT R.N. MURRAY promoted captain and 2/LIEUT MITCHELL promoted LIEUT 2/4/16. Battalion moved to BILLETS at PHILOSOPHE on relief on Battalion in BRIGADE RESERVE.	
PHILOSOPHE WEST	20th APRIL 21st		Battalion in Brigade Reserve.	
"	22nd		2/LIEUT B. WATSON and 2/LIEUT N.H. COLLINS reported for duty at 12-30 p.m. and have been taken on the strength of the Battalion accordingly.	
"	23rd		EASTER SUNDAY. Battalion in Brigade Reserve in PHILOSOPHE. Orders for the Battalion to move from Bole Reserve to Right Sub Sector Hulluch Section received at 11-30 a.m.	
"	24th		Battalion moved at 10 a.m. from PHILOSOPHE to the trenches, and relieved the 8th Royal Inniskilling Fusiliers in the firing line in the Right Sub-Sector of the HULLUCH Section extending from POSEN ALLEY, inclusive to POLLY LANE. 'A' 'B' 'C' coys in the firing line, each forming its own supports with 'D' coy in RESERVE TRENCH. The relief was completed at 2-10 p.m.	
In the field	25th		Situation quite normal.	
"	26th		'D' coy relieved 'A' coy in the firing line at 10 a.m.	

Army Form C. 2118.

WAR DIARY
INTELLIGENCE SUMMARY
(Erase heading not required.)

7th R. Innis K. Fslg Fus

Place	Date	Hour	Summary of Events and Information	Remarks and references to Appendices
Firing Line HULLUCH Right SECTION	27 April 1916		D Coy on Right. B in centre. C on left. A Coy in support in RESERVE TRENCH. Rifles in front line had 2 Platoons firing line, 2 in support.	
		5.05 a.m.	In knife from bombardment commenced by Germans on "firing" & support "trenches" with artillery barrage along 10 Avenue - PONT STREET etc, on a front of about 2500 yards.	
		5.55 a.m.	The bombardment of the front trenches & the Kink. The attack being seriously strong about BERRY AVE, cover of gas attack. The Germans were repulsed throughout our front and the Kink. The Germans were driven back in the first attack, and carried	
		7.40	under cover of a second and even denser gas, them in the first attack and asked to manage to by a strong artillery barrage. The Germans again attacked in front of C & D Coys trenches.	
			effort of Judgment in frank of c & DC Coy trenches. They were immediately counter attacked by Platoons sent up from "A" Coy in support and driven out.	
			The RESERVE. Trenches and Avenues, The Irish Fusiliers (2nd Lieut (left) R. Innis son) were placed at the Pt 22 Guards Pt, a company of the 7 R.I.F. ("A" Coy ("E") in the RESERVE TRENCH.	
		9.20am	Artillery and Infantry fire continued until about 9.20am They 9.50am everything was	
		9.50 am	our front was normal by own.	

Army Form C. 2118.

WAR DIARY
or
INTELLIGENCE SUMMARY.
(Erase heading not required.)

7th R. INNISKILLING. Fus.   No 8

Instructions regarding War Diaries and Intelligence Summaries are contained in F. S. Regs., Part II. and the Staff Manual respectively. Title pages will be prepared in manuscript.

Place	Date	Hour	Summary of Events and Information	Remarks and references to Appendices
Hulluch Right Sub Section	27th April 1916		Casualties on the 27th April were as follows:- Officers:- CAPT. W.H. COLLIS. wounded 27-4-16. " J. RITTY Gassed 27-4-16. 2/LIEUT. N.H. COLLINS. Gassed 27-4-16, and died on the way to hospital. 2/LIEUT F.S. CARRULL Gassed 27-4-16. CAPT. R.N. MURRAY reported missing 27-4-16. LIEUT. E. GALLAGHER Gassed 27-4-16. 2/LIEUT. F.A. MILLIGAN Gassed 27-4-16. CAPT. C.H. Staniforth Gassed 27-4-16. 2/LIEUT. R.T. SUTTON. wounded 27-4-16. But remained at duty.	
	28th April 1916		Battalion relieved by the 8th Royal INNISKILLING Fus on the morning of the 28th April, and took over the SUPPORT LINE from the 7th R. IRISH FUS. Dispositions of the companies were as follows:- 'A' Coy :- POSEN ALLEY to LONE TREE REDOUBT. 'B' Coy :- in RESERVE TRENCH. 'C' Coy :- LONE TREE REDOUBT to HAY ALLEY. 'D' " :- HAY ALLEY to HULLUCH ROAD. Situation during the day quite normal.	
	29th APRIL 1916		at 3.55. a.m. so it appeared to this Battalion, a heavy gun fire was directed by Germans on the QUARRY Section. at 4. a. m. the S.O.S. signal was received from B.D.E, though no gas	

Army Form C. 2118.

WAR DIARY
or
INTELLIGENCE SUMMARY
(Erase heading not required)

7TH R. INNISKILLING Fus. No 9

Place	Date	Hour	Summary of Events and Information	Remarks and references to Appendices
Hulluch Sector	April 29th		was noticeable in 10th AVENUE until 4-10 a.m.	
		4-26 a.m.	O.C. 8th R. INNISKILLINGS, at this time in the firing line, asked for a company of this battalion to support him. C Coy under MAJOR. A. D. REID was sent to the RESERVE TRENCH of 8th R. INNIS Fus.	
		4.55 a.m.	'B' Coy reported that they had been heavily shelled in RESERVE TRENCH.	
		5. a.m.	Enemy's gun fire practically ceased.	
		5-12 a.m.	10th AVENUE practically free from gas, and situation was normal throughout the remainder of the day. Casualties on the 29th APRIL 1916. CAPT. A. C. TAGGART. Severe 29-4-16 but remained at duty. Evacuated for 27th and 29th April amounted to 10 officers and 253 other ranks. out of a total of 27 officers and 603 O.R.s in the trenches. Effects of GAS POISONING recorded on 27-4-16. 2/LIEUT. F. A. MILLIGAN. died from effects of GAS POISONING. The army commander GENERAL SIR CHARLES MUNRO telephoned to congratulate the 49th INF. BDE on their gallant conduct on the morning of the 27th inst. The Divisional commander Major General Hickie also telephoned to say how pleased he is of their behaviour. The above messages apply chiefly to the two battalions of the Brigade in the firing line. Further the trust of the attack would appear to have fallen on the 7th R. of I & INNISKILLING Fus. The Commdg officers received the following personal letter	

WAR DIARY
INTELLIGENCE SUMMARY

7th R. INNISKILLINGS. No 10

Army Form C. 2118.

Place	Date	Hour	Summary of Events and Information	Remarks and references to Appendices
HULLUCH	29th April		From Major General Hickie C.B. commanding the 16th Division. "I am directed by Sir Charles Munro commanding the 1st Army to convey to you and to the officers N.C.O's. and men of the Battalion under your command his appreciation of the conduct of the Battalion on the occasion of the German attack on APRIL 27th & 29th. To these congratulations I wish also to add my own thanks." Orders were received to the effect that the Battalion at 7 P.M. relief was to be relieved by the 9th CAMERONS. Relief was completed at 11 P.M.	
PHILOSOPHÉ	30th April		The Battalion marched into PHILOSOPHÉ for a few day's rest. The following is an extract from Battalion Orders dated 30.4.16. "The Commanding Officer desires on his own behalf to express to all ranks his high appreciation of their conduct and bearing on the 27th and 29th inst. when they displayed a high standard of courage and endurance and showed themselves worthy upholders of the traditions of the Royal INNISKILLING Fusiliers.	
"	1st to 7th May		Battalion in rest in PHILOSOPHÉ. On the afternoon of the 3rd May, Brig. Genl. Pereira - Brown commanding the 49th INF BDE addressed the Battalion and said: "He admired you immensely and the courage you have shown. I met you here before you were in the line, and especially on the	

WAR DIARY
INTELLIGENCE SUMMARY.

(Erase heading not required.) 7th R. INNISKILLING Fus. No 11

Place	Date	Hour	Summary of Events and Information	Remarks and references to Appendices
	27th and 29th April.		The other Battalions of the Brigade get enough of it when they have trouble them. By the fighting you have come through, you have found out one thing, namely, that the Officers you have are good men, whom you can trust, and with them you will get along alright; and at the same time, your Officers have found you men to be such men as you have proved yourselves and men of your country. Colonel can be proud of you, and in future when asked what Battalion did you belong to, you can say with pride you were in the 7th R. INNIS Fus a nice fighting Battalion, and you will not require to say anything further remarks. I am only on you, whenever you "go." I thank you very much.	
PHILOSOPHE	4th MAY 1916.		Battalion marched into the trenches and relieved the 8th K.O.S.B. in 14th avenue. Disposition of Coys as follows:- "A" ... Coy. POSEN ALLEY to LONE TREE. REDOUBT. "B" ... " LONE. TREE. REDOUBT. "C" ... " from LONE. TREE. REDOUBT to HAY ALLEY. "D" ... " HAY ALLEY to HULLUCK. Road.	
	5th 6th MAY.		Situation normal. On the 6th APRIL the battalion was relieved by the 7th R. Irish Rifles. Battalion marched to NOEUX LES MINES gtr. no 7.	

WAR DIARY or INTELLIGENCE SUMMARY

7th R. INNISKILLING Fus. Army Form C. 2118.

NO. 12. VOL 4

Place	Date	Hour	Summary of Events and Information	Remarks and references to Appendices
Noeux LES MINES	7th to 17th		On the 11th MAY at 6-50 p.m. orders received for the battalion to stand by and be ready to move at an hour's notice. Two mules were cancelled on the 12th inst at 11-15 a.m. Battalion training proceeded with. On the 14th inst at 6-30 p.m. orders to move into the trenches again on the night of the 17/18th received. Bn moved from NUEUX-LES-MINES on night 17/18th MAY into the new LOOS-section taking over from Battalions of the 2nd INF BDE and 47th INF BDE in the firing. Dispositions of Coys as follows:- 'B' Coy on the right from NORTH. STREET to GORDON. ALLEY. 'A' " in the centre " GORDON ALLEY to SCOTS. ALLEY. 'C' " on the left " SCOTS. ALLEY to ENGLISH ALLEY. 'D' " in firing line in Support. Each Coy in firing line in cellars NORTH. of SCOTS. ALLEY. 'B' Coy in RESERVE in cellars NORTH of SCOTS. ALLEY.	
	18th		Situation normal.	
	19th		2/LIEUT. S.S. MARK and C. CLARKE reported their arrival and are on the strength accordingly. 2/LIEUT (Temp Capt) d' L'E. BROWNLOW. wounded.	
	20th		'B' Coy relieved 'C' Coy in the firing line. Situation normal.	
In the Quad	21/22nd		Battalion relieved by 8th R. INNISKILLING Fus. and went to SUPPORT LINE. Relief completed at 10-45 p.m. Dispositions of Coys as follows:- 'A' Q 5 and 'A' Coy in the VILLAGE LINE. 'B' Coy in the CELLARS. S. 35 d. 6. 5. 'C' " " " cellars NORTH of SCOTS ALLEY. 'D' " " " " of ENCLOSURE. M. F. G.	

WAR DIARY
or
INTELLIGENCE SUMMARY.

(Erase heading not required.)

Army Form C. 2118.

Place	Date	Hour	Summary of Events and Information	Remarks and references to Appendices
GAZINFARBE	15 & 17th May		Bgtt. Chain in Res. Tubb. MAZINGARBE – weather fine	Lettres
	18th May		Battalion reinforced by draft of 89 men from No 5 Entrenching Battalion, that of these men Lloyds & 1st and 2nd Battalions.	Lettres
	19th May		Officers of 1/D O R Visit trench System by Motor Bus, whole of Battalion to study	
	14/20 May		Battalion moved to 5 trenches and relieved 3 Companies 1/2 Bn. ROYAL SUSSEX REGT in Batt. Subtab LOOS SECTOR. Distribution as follows. Bn HQ(?)	
			VILLAGE LINE near 65 Metal Point Reserved 9.30.D.4.1	
			A Coy in cellars near Pim Pope – G.30.C. 4.7.	
			B " " " N.W. of ENCLOSURE M.5.7.9.12	
			C " " " N. of SCOTS ALLEY. G.36.D.5.7.b	
			D " " in VILLAGE LINE	Lettres
	27/31 May		Casualties kills 1 O.R wounded 5 O.R.	
	24/May 25th May		Battalion moved up and relieved 11th R INNIS. FUS. in LEFT (9th–11th) section LOOS SECTOR	
			Battalion in occupation LEFT SUB Section LOOS SECTOR Battalion HQs as follows:	
			Batt. H.Q cellars at G.36.a.5.7.	
			A Coy in W.Half trench from SCOTS ALLEY exclusive to ENGLISH R. By Alma 6.43.6	
			B " " E Half " " NEW T. ST. incl. to GORDON ALLEY excl	
			C " in reserve cellars and RESERVE TRENCH G.36.D.56.5	
			D " in cellars near home for our POISON MARCI MARINER & SCOTS PALEYARD	Lettres

WAR DIARY   7th R INNISKILLING Fus.

INTELLIGENCE SUMMARY.

No. 13

Army Form C. 2118.

(Erase heading not required.)

Place	Date	Hour	Summary of Events and Information	Remarks and references to Appendices
In the Field	23rd MAY.		Situation normal. Battalion in SUPPORT.	
"	24th/25th		Battalion in SUPPORT. CAPT. C. H. STAINFORTH reported his arrival and assumed command of 'D' Coy. 8th Royal INNISKILLING Fusiliers in the front line left sub sector LOOS.	
"	25th/26th		Battalion relieved 8th Royal INNISKILLING Fusiliers in the front line left sub sector LOOS. Disposition of coys as follows:—	
			'C' coy from NORTH STREET inclusive to GORDON ALLEY exclusive	
			'D' " " GORDON ALLEY " " SCOTS ALLEY "	
			'B' " " SCOTS ALLEY " " ENGLISH ALLEY inclusive.	
			'D' Coy in RESERVE in the cellars NORTH of SCOTS ALLEY.	
			Battalion. H.Q. in "FORT INNISKILLING", LOOS.	
			Relief completed at 1-15 a.m.	
"	26/27th		On night 26/27th 'D' Company moved up to the firing line, thus furnishing wounded by our own coys in the firing line, each forming its own support.	
			16th Div Cyclist Coy were attached to the Battalion, and were placed in the RESERVE LINE	
			Disposition of coys as follows:—	
			'C' coy NORTH STREET inclusive to SEAFORTH ALLEY (exclusive).	
			'D' " SEAFORTH ALLEY " " CAMERON ALLEY "	
			'A' " CAMERON ALLEY " " SCOTS ALLEY "	
			'B' " SCOTS ALLEY " " ENGLISH ALLEY (inclusive).	
			16th DIV CYCLIST COY in Reserve in the cellars NORTH of SCOTS ALLEY.	

Army Form C. 2118.

WAR DIARY
or
INTELLIGENCE SUMMARY
(Erase heading not required.)

Instructions regarding War Diaries and Intelligence Summaries are contained in F. S. Regs., Part II. and the Staff Manual respectively. Title pages will be prepared in manuscript.

Place	Date	Hour	Summary of Events and Information	Remarks and references to Appendices
		10.0 A.m.	Very heavy. Officers killed. Officers Wounded (gas)	
			Lieut. L. Quinlan 27/4/18. 2/Lieut. W. Turner 27/4/18.	
			Lieut. F.P.M. Leonard 29/4/18. Capt. J.E. Knott. 29/4/18	
			Lieut. D. Whelton " Lieut. L.F.A. Constable "	
			2/Lieut. M.D. Trimble " Lieut. W.A. Browne	
			2/Lieut. R.E. Gillett. 2/Lieut. G.H. Mansfield	
			Other ranks – Killed & Died of wounds 57. Wounded 269.	
	29th	8 p.m.	Battalion was relieved by 7th Leinster Regt. and moved into billets in Aubigny ETR.	Webm
	30th	7.30 p.m	Battalion moved back to rest billets at Magnicarbe	Webm
			— End of Month. —	

W.E.N. Vines
"Capt. & Adjutant."
8th (S) Battalion R. Innis. Fusiliers.

Army Form C. 2118.

WAR DIARY

7th Royal INNISKILLING FUS.

INTELLIGENCE SUMMARY.

No 14.

(Erase heading not required.)

Instructions regarding War Diaries and Intelligence
Summaries are contained in F.S. Regs., Part II.
and the Staff Manual respectively. Title pages
will be prepared in manuscript.

Place	Date	Hour	Summary of Events and Information	Remarks and references to Appendices
In the field	26/27th		A special Coy under the command of MAJOR REID composed on under was formed and proceeded to MAZINGARBE for special training. Coy to consist of 1 Officer, 1 Sergt, 10 pt., 15 bombers and 6 bayonet men.	
			B " " 1 " 1 " 10 " " 4 "	
			C " " 1 " 1 " 10 " " 4 "	
			D " " 1 " 1 " 10 " " 4 "	
	27th MAY		Situation normal.	
	28th		Situation normal. Major REID's special Coy returned to the Battalion on the evening of the 28th and took up position in the RESERVE LINE in CRUM N of SCOTS ALLEY.	
			Extract from Battalion Routine Orders No 47 para 306 dated 28-5-16 :-
Parchment certificates have been awarded to the following Officers and O.R's for their services during the attacks on APRIL 27th to 29th 1916 :-	
			MAJOR. R. ROSS-WHITE. CAPT. J. RITTY.	
			" A. D. REID. LIEUT. & A.C. WALKER	
			CAPT. and ADJT. A.C. TAGGART. LIEUT. E.N. FLOOK.	
			LIEUT. G.D. ALLEY (R.A.M.C.) 2/LIEUT. H.B.O. MITCHELL	
			2/LIEUT.(temp.Capt.) R.T. SUTTON. 2/LIEUT. Q.G. TRIMBLE.	
			2/LIEUT (temp.LIEUT) C. LEFEVRE. 13133. a/R.S.M. R. Dolan.	
			2914 a/C.S.M. G. COOMBES. 13445. Sergt. G. DUNNE.	
			16520 CORPL. J.J. McGUINNESS. 22780 L/CPL. C. COCHRANE	
			24180 PTE. G. MAGUIRE. 23618. PTE. H. Smyth	
			25288. PTE. P. BROWN. 22505 PTE. P. BROWN.	
			23325. PTE. H. ROBINSON.	
			The Major General Commdg. 16th Division wishes to convey to these	

WAR DIARY

INTELLIGENCE SUMMARY.

7th Royal Inniskilling Fus:

No 15

Army Form C. 2118.

(Erase heading not required.)

Place	Date	Hour	Summary of Events and Information	Remarks and references to Appendices
In the field	29th May		Officers, N.C.O's and men his appreciation of their behaviour. Situation normal. On the night of the 29th/30th the Battalion was relieved by the 5th Royal Berkshire Regt, and was supporting 'D' coy and one platoon 'A' coy moved to Brigade Reserve billets at PHILOSOPHE EAST. Relief was completed at 12·55 a.m. 'D' coy in the Village line from Railway Alley to Lens Road. 'C' coy (one platoon) in the Lens Road Redoubt. CAPTAIN R.S. Kerr wounded (at duty)	
	30th May 31st		Battalion in Brigade Reserve in PHILOSOPHE. " " " " Unnumeration 2/Lieuts. W. Elvery reported for duty on the 17th and was taken on the strength and posted to 'A' coy " T. Martin " " " 17th " " " " " C " J.S. Knox " " " 17th " " " " " B General Sir Douglas Haig, G.C.B. K.C.I.E. K.C.V.O in his dispatch, dated 19th May 1916, mentioned the Battalion for having done excellent work during the period under review, and specially for good work in carrying out and repelling trench attacks and raids.	

A. Toussaint Capt
7th R.Innis Fus

O/C Lt. 7th R. Innis Fus

7. Inniskilling
Vol 5
of June

2.N.
Eshots

XVI

CONFIDENTIAL.

WAR DIARY.
of
7th (S). Batt. Royal INNISKILLING Fusiliers

from 1st June 1916 to 30th June 1916.

(Volume) to Aug '17

Army Form C. 2118.

WAR DIARY
or
INTELLIGENCE SUMMARY

(Erase heading not required.)

7 R. Royal Inniskilling Fus
No 16

Place	Date	Hour	Summary of Events and Information	Remarks and references to Appendices
PHILOSOPHE	1st June		Battalion in PHILOSOPHE in Brigade Reserve. Orders to move into rest to NOEUX LES MINES received at 9.30 a.m.	Q & T.
" "	2nd "		Battalion in Philosophe. Battalion moved at 4.50 p.m. to relieve 2nd Munster Fusiliers. relieved in PHILOSOPHE by the 1st Royal Munster Fusiliers. D Coy in the VILLAGE LINE relieved by H.Q. and 2 Coys of the 9th Royal and one Platoon 'A' Coy in the LENS ROAD REDOUBT. DUBLIN Fusiliers. The battalion remainder remained in Philosophe East has been reorganized as a regulated burial ground by the Graves Registration Committee. Orders received at 11.15 p.m. to "stand-to", and be ready to move at one hours notice from 9 a.m to 5 p.m, and for remainder of 24 hours to be ready to move at half an hours notice. This order to hold good until further orders. Order was acknowledged at 9 a.m on 3rd June 1916.	Q & T.
" "	3rd "		Battalion in rest and "standing to" as per above order.	
" "	4 "		Battalion in rest. Lieut-General E.T. McM. CAVANAGH, C.V.O. C.B. D.S.O. Commdg. 1st CORPS. presented the following Officers and other ranks with the undermentioned decorations for gallantry and Devotion to duty on the 27th April 1916 during the gas attack at HULLUCH :- LIEUT. H.B.O. MITCHELL . . . . . MILITARY CROSS. PTE. P. BROWN. 'B' Coy . . . " " MEDAL. 22505 " H. ROBINSON. 'D' " . . . " " MEDAL. 23325	Q & T.

Army Form C. 2118.

WAR DIARY
or
INTELLIGENCE SUMMARY. 7th Royal Inniskilling Fus.
No. 17
(Erase heading not required.)

Instructions regarding War Diaries and Intelligence Summaries are contained in F. S. Regs., Part II. and the Staff Manual respectively. Title pages will be prepared in manuscript.

Place	Date	Hour	Summary of Events and Information	Remarks and references to Appendices
Noeux les Mines	4th June		The following Officers and NCO'S went unable to the present, but now the following awards.	O.C.T
			CAPTAIN. J. RITTI ———— MILITARY. CROSS.	
			29114 C.S.M. J. COOMBES. " " MEDAL.	
			MAJOR-GENERAL W.B.HICKIE, C.B. Commands 16th Div. forwarded parchment certificates for the following N.C.O'S for coolness and courageous conduct in entering a mine shaft, after a camouflet had been blown by the enemy, and rescuing gassed men on the night 26/27th May 1916. in the LOOS SECTOR.	
			21108. C.S.M. E. McKERNAN } "C" Coy 7th R. INNIS. Fus.	
			13773. Corporal. J. RAINEY }	
	5th June		Battalion in rest billets. The Commanding Officers inspected the Battalion by companies at turn as stated:-	O.C.T
			'A' Coy ———— 9 a.m.	
			'B' " ———— 11 a.m.	
			'C' " ———— 1-30 p.m.	
			'D' " ———— 3-30 p.m.	
	6th June		Special parade was ordered to enable General Sir Charles Munro G.C.M.G. K.C.B. to inspect the Battalion. The parade was cancelled owing to the weather. 18 officers and 471 other ranks would	O.C.T

T2134. Wt. W708-776. 500000. 4/15. Sir J. C. & S.

Army Form C. 2118.

WAR DIARY
INTELLIGENCE SUMMARY
(Erase heading not required.)

7th Royal INNISKILLING. Fus

No 18

Place	Date	Hour	Summary of Events and Information	Remarks and references to Appendices
Noeux les Mines	6th June		have paraded. The Commdg officer held the parade and presented the 16th Div. parchment certificates as shown in the War Diary on the 28th May 1916 and 4th June 1916.	A 27
"	7th June		Ordinary training otherwise carried out	A 27
"	8th June		Battalion in rest, and "standing to" as per previous order.	
"	9th "		Battalion in rest and "standing to" as per previous order.	
"	10th "		" " " " " " " "	
			" " Moved into the 76/7 Sub Section (VENDIN ALLEY to BOYAU 60. is in immediately N. of the CORALN PIT. A Coy in Reserve Trench	
			B " Centre of front line	
			C " on Right " "	
			D " " 7.2.7b " "	
In the field 11th "			Battalion in the left sub. Section 14 Bde Section. 13th June 1916. CAPT. R.T. SUTTON wounded. 16th June 1916 2/Lieut B. WATSON wounded.	A 27
" 15/16 "			On the night 15/16th June Battalion relieved by the 8th R. INNISKILLING Fus and proceeded into Bivouac Reserve in the VILLAGE LINE.	

WAR DIARY
INTELLIGENCE SUMMARY.
4th Royal Innisk. Lusiliers No 19.

(Erase heading not required.)

Army Form C. 2118.

Place	Date	Hour	Summary of Events and Information	Remarks and references to Appendices
Inkefield	17th June		Dispositions of Coys as follows :- "A" "B" "C" Coys in VILLAGE LINE from junction of VILLAGE LINE with TENTH AVENUE to LONE TRENCH. 2/Lieut B. WATSON died from wounds received on Feb 16th inst at the 33rd Casualty Clearing Station Bethune and buried in Battalion Cemetery Philosophe.	O & T
"	18th June		Battalion in the VILLAGE LINE. Large Fatigues parties furnished on the night 20/21st June Battalion relieved 8th Royal Innis. Fusiliers in the Left Sub Section IL BIS SECTOR. Relief was completed at	O & T
"	to 20/21st June	12-45 a.m	Disposition of Coys as follows:- 'A' Coy from Bayan 60 inclusive to Bayan 64 exclusive. 'B' " " " 64 " " 65 inclusive 'C' " " " 65 inclusive " " 68 " 'D' " " " 68 " " 69 " (VERDIN ALLEY) 'D' Coy 8th R. Irish Fus. was attached to the Battalion and held the Reserve trench as follows:- (a) By day from HUGO LANE to	

Army Form C. 2118.

WAR DIARY
or
INTELLIGENCE SUMMARY.   7th Royal Inniskilling Fus
No 2.0.
(Erase heading not required.)

Instructions regarding War Diaries and Intelligence Summaries are contained in F. S. Regs., Part II. and the Staff Manual respectively. Title pages will be prepared in manuscript.

Place	Date	Hour	Summary of Events and Information	Remarks and references to Appendices
			JENDIN ALLEY.	
			(b) By night (i.e. from 8 p.m to 6 a.m) from about 40 yards North of POSEN ALLEY to VENDIN ALLEY inclusive. Battalion H.Q's in CURZON STREET.	O.E.T
			On the 18th inst 49th Inf Bde. informed the C.O. by wire that 21108 C/S.Major E. McKernan and 13373 Corpl. Rainey had been awarded the MILITARY Medal for gallantry on the 26th/27th May 1916 in the LOOS SECTOR.	
In the field	21st June		CAPT. A. E. TAGGART wounded at duty. 2/LIEUT. A. E. E. TRIMBLE wounded. On the night of the 21st fatigue parties found for closing assembly trenches denus BROADWAY.	O.E.T
"	22/23rd		On the night 22/23rd June battalion relieved by the 8th Royal INNISKILLING Fus. Relief completed at 11.30 p.m 22nd June 1916. Battalion moved into Brigade Support in 10th division. Dispositions were as follows:—	O.E.T

T2134. Wt. W708—776. 500000. 4/15. Sir J. C. & S.

WAR DIARY or INTELLIGENCE SUMMARY

Army Form C. 2118.

7th Royal Inniskilling Fus. No 2.

Place	Date	Hour	Summary of Events and Information	Remarks and references to Appendices
In the field	22/23rd		'A' Coy were held from 200 yards S. of CHALK PIT ALLEY inclusive to N. SAP. REDOUBT. (exclusive)	
			'B' Coy less 1 platoon N. SAP. REDOUBT exclusive to POSEN ALLEY inclusive	
			1 platoon 'B' Coy in N. SAP. REDOUBT.	O.e.T
			'C' " POSEN ALLEY exclusive to PONT ST. inclusive.	
			'D' " PONT. ST. " to VENDIN ALLEY "	
			Batt. H.Q's on the right in South of 'A' Coy.	
	24th		Situation normal. Battalion employed on strengthened parapets in 10th AVENUE	O.e.T
	25th		C.O. met the Brigadier 49th Inf Bde at H.Q's of 2/7 R. Inns. Holding the in BURTON ST. Battalion ordered to do a raid in section allotted by Brigadier 49th Inf Bde, namely between BYRNE 67 and 68. Smoke Candles, P. Bombs, and discharge of Jam Wallets to be used to cover the raiding party. Gas Stand pipes East Stand pipe was allotted as D.C. Raiding party, and was assisted by the following officers :— Lieut. H.B.D. MITCHELL 2/Lieut. J. Cunningham CROWE and SHAW. 2/Lt. E.S.M. McKernan Raiding party left 10th Avenue at 11-15 p.m to take up their	O.e.T " KNIBBS.

WAR DIARY
of
INTELLIGENCE SUMMARY.

Army Form C. 2118.

7th Royal Inniskilling Fus. No 22

Place	Date	Hour	Summary of Events and Information	Remarks and references to Appendices
Iwuy field	June 26		Position in Support line between Bayou 67 and 68. At 11-50 p.m. message received from 49 INF. BDE that the raid was cancelled. At 11-52 p.m. message sent to Capt. STAINFORTH that the raid was cancelled and gun orders to bring back the party having been given in 10M Avenue. On the morning of the 26th June 1916 at 10 a.m. Battalion relieved by 7th Royal IRISH RIFLES, and marched into Billets in MAZINGARBE. Relief completed at 12-10 p.m.	O.E.T.
MAZINGARBE	June 27		Battalion in rest in billets at MAZINGARBE. Fatigue parties being found.	O.E.T.
	28 June		The Commdg. Officer attends a conference at 49th INF BDE. Office at 5-30 p.m. re training and General work of the Battalion.	O.E.T.
	29th "		Battalion in rest in MAZINGARBE. Furnishing fatigues.	O.E.T.
	30th "		Battalion in billets. The Commdg. Officer attends a conference at 49th Inf. Bde. H.Q's at 10-30 a.m regarding huming Battalion in Burlock Reserve in mazingarbe.	O.E.T.

WAR DIARY

7th (S) Battln
Royal Inniskilling Fus

1st. July to 31st. July 1916.

VOLUME No. 6

Army Form C. 2118.

WAR DIARY
or
INTELLIGENCE SUMMARY.
(Erase heading not required.)

7th Royal Inniskilling Fus.

No 23

Instructions regarding War Diaries and Intelligence Summaries are contained in F. S. Regs., Part II. and the Staff Manual respectively. Title pages will be prepared in manuscript.

Place	Date	Hour	Summary of Events and Information	Remarks and references to Appendices
MAZINGARBE	1st July 1916.		Battalion in huts in MAZINGARBE in Brigade Reserve. Special Company under the command of Major A.D. REID came in, hand grenades for raiding purposes. Orders re move to the line received from 49th INF. BDE. received at 6.30 P.M.	
" "	2nd July 1916.		Battalion in huts in Brigade Reserve. Operation Orders re move to Brigade Support LOOS SECTOR issued to all concerned at 5.30 p.m.	
" "	3rd July 1916.		Battalion left MAZINGARBE at 10 a.m. for the trenches. Battalion in Brigade Support of the LOOS SECTOR. Disposition of Coys as follows:— a Coy in cellars of ENCLOSURE. B " " " P.I.P. ST. (attached to 8th B. knows two for tactical purposes) D " " " " " " " " " " " (" " " " " ") C " " " DUKE STREET. Battalion Headquarters in DUKE ST.	
	4th to 7th		Battalion in Brigade Support. Orders received from Brigade HQrs on the 6th inst at 6.30 P.M. to relieve the 8th R. Innis. Fus. in the front line LEFT SUB SECTOR LOOS on the night 7/8th inst.	
	8th July		Battalion relieved the 8th Royal INNISKILLING FUS. in the LEFT SUB SECTOR LOOS	

WAR DIARY

INTELLIGENCE SUMMARY — 7th Royal INNISKILLING Fus'rs

Army Form C. 2118.

Place	Date	Hour	Summary of Events and Information	Remarks and references to Appendices
Martinsart	9th July		Reliefs completed at 12.45 a.m. Disposition of Coys as follows:—	
			'C' Coy from NORTH ST. to JORDAN ALLEY inclusive	
			'B' " " JORDAN ALLEY to SCOTS ALLEY "	
			'C' " " SCOTS ALLEY to ENGLISH ALLEY "	
			'D' " in the RESERVE LINE between PIP ST.	
			Two coys of the 7th R. Irish Fus'rs attached as support Coy for fatigue purposes.	
			'A' Coy 7th R. Irish Fus'rs in DUKE ST.	
			'B' " " " " in ELBOW & of PIP ST.	
	10th		Situation normal.	
			2/Lieut J.S. KNOX wounded in the stomach by Shrapnel. Major R. ROSS-WHITE sent to ENGLAND "sick" 29th June 1915 and struck off the strength of the battalion with effect from 30th June 1916. Authy. 16th Div No. 6750/75 d. 10-7-16.	
			2/Lieut J.S. KNOX died of wounds received in action on 10th July 1916 at 33rd CAS. C.L.G. STN and was buried in PHILOSOPHE EAST in the Battalion Cemetery.	
	11th		2/Lieut M. ELVERY wounded, by three hostile bombs causing it to explode and splitting sandbags behind his arm. Bombs issued at 9.30 p.m. from Batt.	

WAR DIARY
INTELLIGENCE SUMMARY

Army Form C. 2118.

7th Royal INNISKILLING Fus. No 2 S

(Erase heading not required.)

Instructions regarding War Diaries and Intelligence Summaries are contained in F.S. Regs., Part II. and the Staff Manual respectively. Title pages will be prepared in manuscript.

Place	Date	Hour	Summary of Events and Information	Remarks and references to Appendices
In the Field	11th July		Strength that the battalion would be relieved by 8th R. INNISKILLING Fus. on night 11/12th inst. Capt PARR and a party of 10 men raided a Hun post at 1.0 a.m. (Between SEAFORTH CRATER & UNSTON CRATER) It was reported the same was unoccupied. Raid was with a good success.	
	12th		Battalion relieved by 8th R. Inniskilling Fus. at 3 p.m. Battalion marched into billets, except "B" Coy, in PHILOSOPHE EAST, in Brigade Reserve. "B" Coy. in the VILLAGE LINE, also finding garrison of LENS ROAD REDOUBT	
	13th		Battalion finding garrison.	
	14th		Battalion in Brigade Reserve in PHILOSOPHE EAST. Inniskillings finding garrison. Battalion warned at 5.30 PM that the Battalion would relieve the 8th R. Inniskillings Fus. in the firing line left Sub-Sector Loos. Orders for the relief issued to Coys and all coys moved at 10.15 PM except "B" Coy in the village line and garrison of Lens Road Redoubt. "C" Coy relieves "B" Coy in Battalion Reserve in PHILOSOPHE EAST.	
	15th		Relief at 12.10 P.M.	
	16th		The Battalion relieves 8 R Innis Fus as above.	
	17th		} In the trenches. Lieut (Lunch (Act)) R.N. MURRAY reported missing up to 27/1/16. now hold to have died in a German field hospital at CARVIN on 16.28.18.16	
	18th		} Relieved by the 1.R. Innis Fus. 4 BW 7n7. 16th and moved into NOEUX les MINES.	
	19th			
	20th		(While in Divisional Reserve) Return of the 115 A+S H. 45th In 7. & the 15th Div. in the centre Sub Section HULLUCH Sector. Information received that Capt (Lunch) R.N. MURRAY had been taken Prisoner by the Germans on the 27/6/6/16 & that he had died in the field hospital in the CARVIN on 4.7.1916	B.R 27/7/511 B.14/7/511

353 Wt. W3541/1454 700,000 5/15 A.D.S.S./Forms/C. 2118.

WAR DIARY
INTELLIGENCE SUMMARY

Army Form C. 2118.

7th R. Inniskilling Fus.
July 1916

Place	Date	Hour	Summary of Events and Information	Remarks and references to Appendices
Trouilles	22/7/16		Relieved by the 1st & 13th R.M.F. returned into Noeux Puits.	
NOEUX	26/7/16		2 /L: W. HAMILTON 2/L: J.T. FLANNIGAN } 3rd Bn. from Rangers posted to arrival 15/75 2/L: W.T. SMITH 2/L: J.R. MOORE	
	26		} In Huts at NOEUX	
	27			
	28		2 /L: J.J. B ZENN — 12th R Innis Fus " " M.H. WOODS 6 " " " " " H.G. POTTER 5 " " " " " J.R. McCAMBRIDGE 3 " " " reported their arrival were taken on the Strength 29/7/16.	2/L: C.W.D. WALKER 3 R Innis Fus " " T.E. JOHNSTON 6 " " " " " J.S. FOLEY 3 " " " " " H.V. LOWRY 3 " " "
	29			
	30			
	31st		Relieved the 7th Leinster Regt. at 7p7 Rte in PHILOSOPHE.W. 14 Bis Section, Capt. & Adj: A.E. Taggart evacuated from 1st Corps Rest Stn to 1st Cas: Clearing 67 "	

31 July 1916.

A.H. Young Lt Col
7 R. Innis. Fus.

Observations

(1) The enemy machine gun firing from the NORTH had full play all the time.
Our Machine Gun to the N of GORDON ALLEY was out of action & therefore could not bring flanking fire to bear on the enemy when they attacked.

(2) Great difficulty was experienced in digging the NORTH Sap owing to wire being buried. Wire cutters should be in possession of diggers in future.

(3) Owing to unforeseen circumstances there was a shortage of bombs at the NORTH Sap. This was probably due to the original carrying party, when wounded, leaving their bombs where they were at the time.

16/7/16

Received from OC 8th R. Innis
Fus.

3 German Rifles
1 Pack, containing
   Ground Sheet
   Shirt
   3 Pkts Tobacco
   3 rounds SAA
   1 Iron Ration + Sugar
   Mess Tin.

Captured near SEAFORTH CRATER
in raid, night 15/16th July 1916.
Remainder of spoil was handed
to Intelligence Officer + receipt obtained.

BRIGADE MAJOR 49th BRIGADE.

Army Form C. 2118.

WAR DIARY
or
INTELLIGENCE SUMMARY.
(Erase heading not required.)

Place	Date July	Hour	Summary of Events and Information	Remarks and references to Appendices
			The following officers joined during month	
PHILOSOPHE	16th		CAPT. C. SENIER returned from Hospital wounded	6.94 p.m
NOEUX-LES MINES	23rd		2/LT. L.W.L. LEADER } from 4th Bn. CONNAUGHT RANGERS.	6/23 p.m
			" D.C. O'CONNELL	
			" J.A. DIGNAN	
			" J.J. BRUEN	
	29th		2/LT. E.M. SHAW from 5th R. Innis Fus	
			" W.A. CAMPBELL from 5th R. Irish Fus	
			" S.B. COGHILL from 5th R. Innis Fus	
			" J.A. HUNTER do	
			" R.E. PURDY do	
			" L.F.D. MacDOUGALD from 6th R. Innis Fus	6/28 p.m
			" R.F. CASEY reinforcement of new Batt.	

H. O'Halpin Ellenulf Lieut. Col.
Commanding 8th Royal Innis Killing Fus.

Vol 7

WAR DIARY.

7th Royal Inniskilling Fusiliers

MONTH OF AUGUST, 1916.

VOLUME :- 7

WAR DIARY

August 1916.

Army Form C. 2118.

7th Serv. Bn. R. Inniskilling Fus.
Page 27

INTELLIGENCE SUMMARY

Place	Date	Hour	Summary of Events and Information	Remarks and references to Appendices
Augt PHILOSOPHE W	Aug 1.		In Brigade Reserve. Capt: D.H. MORTON returns and is T/A/Adjt vice Capt: T.A. Ady = Act T/Adjutant. 2 Lieut AF C Trimble took over temporary command of "A" Coy	B.R.O 634 B.R.O 634 d. 29/7/16
			2/Lt J. COLLEN 27th 9pm an interview prior to joining the R.F.C.	B.R.O 633 d. 29/7/16
	2		"	
	3		2/Lieuts A.E.C. TRIMBLE J CUNNINGHAM T.H. SHAW R.C. HUGHES A.A. SEWARD granted the rank of Lieutenant in the Brigade without pay. both with effect from the 3/8/16	B.R.O 670 d. 3/8/16 ↳ R/570 d. 1/5/16
			The Temporary promotion of the 7/Lt 7/7/ viz of 7/Lieus cancelled (with rank without pay)	
			Lieut temp Capt: R M MURRAY 27.4.16 " " " A.L.'E BROWN 9.6.16 2 Lieut " " R.T SUTTON 26.8.16 " " " S.L. Henderson 16.5.16	B.R.O 671 d. 3/8/16 + R/1128/1 d. 1/5/16
			2 Lieut H MAGUIRE. 3rd Conn. Rang; Posted to the Bn. Showing to total strength? posted to B Coy	B.R.O 673 d. 3/8/16
	4		Moved into the 27th Sub Section 14 Bde Section in relief of the 8 R Irish No 3	D.O's 2439 d. 3/8/16

Army Form C. 2118.

WAR DIARY
or
INTELLIGENCE SUMMARY.

August 1916. 7th Service Bn R. Innis Fus. Page 26.

(Erase heading not required.)

Place	Date	Hour	Summary of Events and Information	Remarks and references to Appendices
Left Sub Sect	Aug 5		In the Foundry	
	6		"	
	7		"	
14 B/S SECTION	8		Capt. H.V. Parr rejoined from Hospital & took over command of "A" Coy again	D.D.& D d 7/8/16
			Relieved by the 8 R. Innis Fus. & 8th R.D.F. and moved into 10th Avenue, on	
			B.U. support.	
10th AV:	9		Building Huts "B" H.Q's at G 28 C.1.5 in the O.B.Line. 2/Lt W Morgan rejoined his	A.R.O's 859 d 11/8/16
"	10		arrival on 9/8/16 with a batch of men: in the Reg.t from a hospital Lord Stratton Rose	
"	11			
	12	6pm	relieved 8 R Innis Fus in the Left Right Sub Section 14 B/S Sector	O.O.41 d. 11/8/16.
	13		2/Lieut J.S. Glenn "C" Coy wounded by a Rifle Grenade about midst	
			Reorganization of B/g's completed. each Coy detachment of two having being 4	B.R.O 9 05 d. 13/8/16
			formed. The two HQ detachments 4.O.to be formed, numbering 57 guns 7 nil reducing	
			one NCO on establishment.	
	14		In the Foundry	
	15		ditto.	
			9nay R.R Smith & Hospital into Regt.	
			Capt. J. Ritty " " "	
	16		Relieved by the 8th R. Innis Fus moved into the Northern Theels MAZINGARBE	O.O.42 d 15/8/15

Army Form C. 2118.

WAR DIARY
or
INTELLIGENCE SUMMARY. 7 R. Inniskilling Fusiliers
(Erase heading not required)

August 1916   Page 24

Place	Date	Hour	Summary of Events and Information	Remarks and references to Appendices
MAZINGARBE	17		Capt. J.R. Itty took over command vhy 37°C.M. from Lieut. Lefeurr.	B.R.O 711 of 19/8/16
			Maj: R.R. White u/with a Pro: duty at B.M. H.Q's as an assistant.	R.A. 0710 d. 17/8/16
			2/Lieut M.G. PORTER R. B.R. Inniss Fus: attached this Bn: returns Tovral to the B.R. Inniss =	B.R.O 729 d. 19/8/16
"	18		u/with M.G. from the 5/8/16.	
"	19			
"	20		Relieved 8th R. Innis Fus: in the R. 6 + 2 SECT: 14 BIS SECTION	
"	21			
"	22			
"	23			
"	24			
"	25		Relieved by the S.E. Lewis Regt Thomas L no Fux.	O.O. 844 d. 24/8/16
"	26		received admath of 1170 men. March'd to LAPUGNOY.	B.R.O 769.25/8/16 O.D 45 d. 25/8/16
"	27 28		In Billets LAPUGNOY.	I.O. 46 d. 27/8/16
"	29		Moved by Train to LONGNEAU, extraining at FOUQUEROIL	

WAR DIARY or INTELLIGENCE SUMMARY

(Erase heading not required.)

Army Form C. 2118.

Page 30

Aug. 1916   7 R. Inniskilling Fus:

Place	Date	Hour	Summary of Events and Information	Remarks and references to Appendices
LATUGNOY	28.		2/Lieut J.S. FOLEY relieved Capt D.H. MORTON as acting Adjt on the 27th inst.	R.W.770 dt 27/8/16.
"	28		Capt G.D.F. MCy R.A.M.E returned to duty with the Batt'n from the morning. Bn went for a 9 mile route march in the morning. (5 miles)	
VAUX-SUR-SOMME	29		Moved 57H at 6 PM for LONGEVEAL where Bn entrained at 9.10 P.M. arrived LONGUEVAL from AMIENS 5.30. detrained & marched to VAUX SUR SOMME (15 miles) and there came under the orders of the XIV Corps.	
GTE.	30		In billets VAUX. Captain MORTON admitted to Hospital with high temperature.	
GIBRALTAR near BRAY SUR SOMME	31.		Moved by route march 9 miles to GIBRALTAR. Bn entrained withdraw (including Capt ALLEY, R.A.M.C) & 658 O.R.'s. Strength 34 Officers	

1/Sept. 1916.

W.H. Young Lt
7 R. Inniskilling Fus.

WAR DIARY

7b/ Royal Inniskilling Fusiliers

FOR MONTH OF SEPTEMBER, 1916.

VOLUME 8

Army Form C. 2118.

WAR DIARY
or
INTELLIGENCE SUMMARY.
(Erase heading not required.)

7 R INNIS: FUS:

September

Page 31

Place	Date	Hour	Summary of Events and Information	Remarks and references to Appendices
GIBRALTAR CAMP	B.7.b 1.		GIBRALTAR CAMP. HAPPY VALLEY. 19m.17. N 27b.RAY SUN 7 SOMME	
CITADEL N. BRAY-SUR-SOMME	2 3½ 3		The Batt. moves to the CITADEL at 9 a.m. The Batt. moves to BILLON FARM at 9 P.M.	
BILLON FARM				
SEUZE WOOD	night 4th/5th		The Batt. relieved the 12th R.B. in the neighbourhood of SEUZE WOOD dispositions 'A' Coy in SEUZE WOOD B Coy on GINCHY – WEDGE WOOD RD. D Coy " C Coy on GUILLEMONT – SEUZE WOOD RD.	
	5th		Capt C.H. Stanford commdg 'D' Coy was wounded in the arm by shrapnel. 2nd Lt C.A. Crout assumes command 'D' Coy.	
	6th	about 6 a.m.	Col. H.N. Young was severely wounded in the leg by a sniper while visiting the front line, at the moment he was talking to Capt F. Ashton commdg 'B' Coy. Major A.D. Reid assumes command of Batt.	

WAR DIARY
INTELLIGENCE SUMMARY
(Erase heading not required.)

Army Form C. 2118.

Place	Date	Hour	Summary of Events and Information	Remarks and references to Appendices
	6th		At 8 p.m. a report was received from 'A' Coy. that the Germans were attacking in BEUZE WOOD. Soon afterwards Capt. Parr. comdg 'A' Coy. reported "all well". Counter attack repulses. 'A' 'D' Coy were moved up to S.W. corner of GEUZE WOOD to support & support 't' coy left flank.	
	Night 6/7th 7th		Major A.D. REID was slightly wounded in the back. C.S.M. Dolan was also wounded at the same time. Capt. R.A. Kerr comdg 'B' Coy around command of Batt. C.S.M. Coombes was appointed actg. R.S.M. Batt. was relieved by 4th London Regiment & proceeded to Div. Reserve at BERNAFAY WOOD	
			2nd Lt. S.S. Foley actg. ADJt. was evacuated, sick. 2nd Lt. A.B. Seward was appointed actg. Adj.	
	Night 7/8th		Capt. V.H. Parr was evacuated suffering from a slight wound received the day before.	
	8		The Batt. moves into GUILLEMONT as Div Reserve.	
GUILLEMONT	Night 8/9			
attack on GINCHY	9th		During the morning orders was received from the Bde. leaving Batt. under orders of 47th Bde. a to get in touch with C.O. 6th R.I.R.	
		4.45 pm	The 47th Bde attacked on the night of GINCHY but were held up by M/G fire	

Army Form C. 2118.

WAR DIARY
or
INTELLIGENCE SUMMARY.
(Erase heading not required.)

Instructions regarding War Diaries and Intelligence Summaries are contained in F. S. Regs., Part II. and the Staff Manual respectively. Title pages will be prepared in manuscript.

Place	Date	Hour	Summary of Events and Information	Remarks and references to Appendices
	9th	4.50	The Batt moved up into support of 47th Bde & came under orders of C.O. 6th R.I.R. The 48th Bde on the left advanced + took GINCHY. The Casualties in the Batt were as follows	
			Capt J. Ritty missing	
			2 Lt A.C. Crowe Killed	
			2 Lt J.R. More "	
			2 Lt W. Morgan "	
			2 Lt H Maguire "	
			Total Casualties 4 Officers killed 1 missing 18 + 4 O.Rs Killed wounded + missing	
	night 9/10		The Batt was relieved by the Guards & proceeds to transport lines BILLON FARM.	
	10th		Major K.C. Weldon Roy. Ir. Fus. attached 7th R. Irish Fus. assumed command of the Batt. Capt R.K. Kerr took over the duties of 2 i/c in command.	
	11th		The Battn moves into billets in SAILLY LE SEC.	

Army Form C. 2118.

WAR DIARY
or
INTELLIGENCE SUMMARY.

September.

Place	Date	Hour	Summary of Events and Information	Remarks and references to Appendices
SAILLY L SEC.	18th		Batty moves into billets at BAILLEUL near ABBEVILLE	
BAILLEUL	20th		Batty moves by train to BERTHEM, 20 miles S YPRES.	
BERTHEM	23rd		Batty moves into the Trenches, relieving the 38th CANADIAN Inf. occupying position N.29-1 to N.29-4. Batt. #62. lying in FORT VICTORIA.	
KEMMEL SHELTERS.	27th		The Batty was relieved by the 7th & 8th R. Irish Fusiliers & came into billets at KEMMEL SHELTERS.	

2353 Wt. W25H/1454 700,000 5/15 D. D. & L. A.D.S.S./Form:/C. 2118.

7th (s) Bn. R. Inniskilling Fusiliers.

Report on operations carried out by the Bn. during the afternoon of the 9th September.

------:------

1. Bt 2 a.m. on 9th the Bn. had taken up its positions in GUILLEMONT as ordered (positions shown on sketch) Coy. Commanders immediately reconnoitred forward position to be taken up on WEDGEWOOD-GINCHY ROAD.
Situation reported to RECITE at 1.45 a.m.

2. During the morning a wire was received from RECITE placing the Battalion under orders of RAKE and to get in touch with C.O. RANDOM - this was accomplished at 3.37 p.m.

3. Two Vickers guns of the 49th Machine Gun Corps were situated as follows:- 1 near CEMETERY, other at point T.19.c.9.8.

4. At 4.50 p.m. Battn. moved to forward position in WEDGE WOOD, GINCHY Rd as ordered by the 49th Bde., no orders having been received from RAKE. When the Battalion reached this position they found the trench still occupied by troops of the Leinsters, Connaughts, Hants & Machine Gun of the R.I.R. Some of the Btn. entered the trench and the remainder dug themselves in behind. This led to great confusion as our men got mixed up with other troops. It is not clear why these troops did not advance in support of the troops in front. Instead of this the 7th Inniskillings were ordered to advance while these troops were left behind. It was very difficult to pick our men from amongst the others.

5. Captain RITTY immediately on arrival at this position got in touch with O.C. RANDOM, who ordered him to "Stand Fast" for the present. Situation wired to RAKE & RECITE at 5.37 p.m.

6. Soon afterwards Captain RITTY was ordered by O.C. RANDOM to support troops in front. He led forward as many men of the 7th as he could disintegrate from the other troops - about 3 companies. The whole line was not ordered to advance; Capt. RITTY did not reach the front line and has since been missing. Lt. MITCHELL took charge, when he reached the front line he found the front trench full of Connaughts, Munsters, Hants & some other troops. These troops appeared to be hopelessly mixed up - Mr. Mitchell reported to the senior officer present who said they had attacked but were driven back by M.G. fire which was deadly, and that the German trench was full of Germans untouched by our artillery. Mr. Mitchell asked for orders and was told to get into an assembly trench just in rear, which he did, with as many of his men as he could collect as by this time they had got mixed up with other troops.
Situation reported to RAKE & RECITE at 6.30 p.m.

7. One company on the right under 2/Lt. RUDDOCK got in touch with the 12 Londons on the right. The officer in charge said they had advanced and had been cut to pieces and only a few remained. Soon afterwards they retired. Mr. RUDDOCK dug in and consolidated the trench and held it until relieved by the Guards.

8. A message from Mr. Mitchell received at 9.04 p.m. stated that he was in touch with the O.C. RANDOM, who was satisfied with his position and he was to stand fast.

9. From the very beginning the Battn. got mixed up with the units of the 47th Bde. holding trenches in front. Instead of the whole line advancing I had to try to disintegrate the 7th Inniskgs. and get them forward, which was very difficult.

10. One Company supported the Leinsters, with whom I was in constant touch during the whole operations. Their 2nd in command I/C was very anxious that I should support his left flank which I did with one company. He feared the safety of GUILLEMONT if counter attacked.

11. The morale of the Battalion was excellent.

12. Communications with RAKE & RECITE were kept up during the whole operations - 5 times the wire to the advanced Brigade Station was cut to pieces but each time a new wire was got out within ten minutes. Communication with Companies was kept up by Battn. and Company runners.

13. The Battn. was relieved by the Guards about 3 a.m.

14. Total casualties number 4 Officers killed, 1 missing, about 100 O.Rs. killed, wounded and missing. The Battn. reached their present camp about 9 a.m.

(Sd) R.G. KEIR Capt.

Commanding 7th (S) Battn.Roy.Innis.Fus.

10/9/16
6.30 p.m.

WAR DIARY

MONTH OF OCTOBER, 1916.

VOLUME 9

7th Royal Inniskilling Fusiliers.

Army Form C. 2118.

WAR DIARY
or
INTELLIGENCE SUMMARY.
(Erase heading not required.)

OCTOBER

A. 35

Place	Date	Hour	Summary of Events and Information	Remarks and references to Appendices
KEMMEL SHELTERS	3/10/16		Relieved 8th R. Irish Fus. in Right Sub-Section. Disposed as follows: "A" & "B" Coys. were in front line, "C" coy in strong points & H.Q, "D" coy in reserve.	
	3/10/16		Lt. Morton (Capt. in Bde) wounded in hand & sniper	
	9/10/16		Relieved by 8th R. Irish Fus & moved to KEMMEL SHELTERS	
	14/10/16		Lt. Col. Weldon went on leave, Capt. Rylden took on temporary command of R.I.R. Batt.	
	14/10/16		Relieved 8th R. Irish Fus. in the Right Sub-section. Coys were disposed as follows: "C" & "D" Coys in front line, "A" coy in strong points & H.Q, "B" coy in reserve	
	17/10/16		The following temporary promotions were made in R.I.R. Batt. Capt. Rylden to be Major while a/c in command. 2nd Lts. Routledge, Tazwell, Cunningham to be Capts. while commanding Coys.	

Army Form C. 2118.

WAR DIARY
or
INTELLIGENCE SUMMARY.
(Erase heading not required.)

Instructions regarding War Diaries and Intelligence Summaries are contained in F. S. Regs., Part II. and the Staff Manual respectively. Title pages will be prepared in manuscript.

Place	Date	Hour	Summary of Events and Information	Remarks and references to Appendices
LOCRE.	21/10/16	—	Relieved by 8th R. INNIS Fus & went into billets at LOCRE	
"	26/10/16		Relieved the 8th R.I. INNIS Fus in the Right Sub Sector. Coys were distributed as follows:— Front line, 'A' Coy on right 'B' Coy on left. 'C' Coy Strong Points 8 & 9 'D' Coy in Reserve.	
	29/10/16		Lt. Col. Weldon left Batt & takes over command of 7/8th R. Irish Fus.	
	29/10/16		Major Plunkett assumes Temporary command of the Batt Vice Lt Col. Weldon	

Plunkett Major
comdg 7/8 R. Innis Fus.

WAR DIARY.

FOR

MONTH OF NOVEMBER, 1916.

VOLUME 10

7th R. Inniskilling Fusiliers

7th R. Innisskilling Fus

WAR DIARY or INTELLIGENCE SUMMARY

Army Form C. 2118.

Place	Date	Summary of Events and Information	Remarks and references to Appendices
LOCRE	1/11/16	Relieves by the 8th R. INNIS FUS in the R.E. Sub. Sector & went into Huts at LOCRE.	
"	6/11/16	The Batt. relieves the 8th R.I. Innisskilling Fus in H. Right Sub. Sector.	
	12/11/16	The Batt. was relieved by the 8th R. Innis Fus & moves into Div. Reserve at LOCRE.	
	18/11/16	The Batt. relieves the 8th R. Innis Fus in H. Right Sub Sector	
	22/11/16 6 p.m	The Batt. in conjunction with 2nd R. Irish Reg. carried out a Dummy Raid on enemy's front line from SPAN BROEKMOLEN to PECKHAM. A Smoke cloud was sent over at zero (6 p.m) — 3 minutes, the enemy mistaking it for gas. At zero our Artillery puts an intense barrage of 18 Pounders & 4.5″ Howitzers on enemy front line after 2 minutes barrage lifted to their support line for 5 minutes. Then back to front line for 2 minutes. The operation was entirely successful.	
	24/11/16	The Batt. was relieved by the 8th R. Innis Fus & moves into Div. Reserve at LOCRE.	R/5/Lieut Maynard 7th Innis Fus

Army Form C. 2118.

WAR DIARY
or
INTELLIGENCE SUMMARY.

(Erase heading not required.)

7th Bde Royal Inniskilling Fusiliers

Instructions regarding War Diaries and Intelligence Summaries are contained in F. S. Regs., Part II. and Staff Manual respectively. Title pages will be prepared in manuscript.

Place	Date	Hour	Summary of Events and Information	Remarks and references to Appendices
LO GRE	24/11/15		Major W.B. Rothwell, R.E Inniskilling Fusiliers reported his arrival & assumed the duties of Acting 2nd in Command.	
"	28/11/15		Major R.G. Kerr proceeded on leave. Major W.B. Rothwell assumed Temporary command of Bn.	
"	30/11/15		The N.F.s relieved the 9th N.F Inniskilling Fusiliers in right sub sector.	

W.B. Rothwell Major
Comdg 7 Bn 1st Inniskilling Fusiliers

2353 Wt. W2514/1454 700,000 5/15 D.D. & L. A.D.S.S./Form/C. 2118.

SECRET.   Copy No.

8th R. Innis. Fus., Operation Order No. 28 – 30/8/16.

1. The Battalion will entrain at PONT REMY, complete with Transport, baggage & supply wagons on 31st inst..

2. Time of Departure of train – 3.40 p.m.
   Train will be of usual composition – "Typ. Combattant."

3. Transport complete, a loading party of 15 O.R. per Coy., under 2/Lieut. J.E. WOODS and A.G. PORTER, will move off at 11.30 p.m. and arrive at entraining station at 12.30 p.m.
   Remainder of Battalion will march to Entraining Station in order, H.Q., "A" "B" "C" "D" Coys..
   Starting Point – Cross Roads – West end of VILLAGE.
   Head of column to pass Starting point – 1.30 p.m.

4. Billeting party composed as under will move off at 11.15 p.m. 30th inst., and will travel with the R. Innis. Fus., in first train leaving PONT REMY at 0.30 a.m. on 31st inst..
      2/Lt. R.E. PILGREM.
      Interpreter.
      C.Q.M. Sergt.
      1 N.C.O. Hd. Qrs..
   This party will take bicycles, and will carry two days' rations. A representative will be detailed to meet the Battalion on arrival at detraining station.

5. Dinners on 31st inst., will be at 10.45 a.m.
   A hot meal will be served at station.

6. Officers' valises, and Mess kits will be dumped at Coy. H.Q., ready for loading at 10 a.m.
   All Transport to be loaded by 10.30 a.m.

7. Billets will be cleaned and all kits outside by 12.30 p.m.
   Certificates to be rendered as to cleanliness of billets, and that all water bottles are filled.

8. Water carts will travel filled.

9. The usual orders for entraining, detraining and train discipline will be observed.

10. Train Guards will be detailed as follows:-
    H.Q. 1 N.C.O. & 12 O.R. to mount at front of train and do duty on right side of train.
    Officer for duty with this Guard – 2/Lieut. L.G.B. McDOUGALD.

    "D" Coy. 1 N.C.O. and 12 O.R. to mount at rear of train and do duty on left side of train.
    Officer for duty with this Guard – 2/Lieut. J.P. DICKSON.

11. Acknowledge.

                                                     Capt. & Adjt..
                                                     8th R. Innis. Fus...

Copy No. 1 to O.C. "A" Coy.,
   "   " 2 "   "   "B" "
   "   " 3 "   "   "C" "
   "   " 4 "   "   "D" "
   "   " 5 " Signalling Officer.
   "   " 6 " Quartermaster.
   "   " 7 " Transport Officer.
   "   " 8 " Medical Officer.
   "   " 9 " 2/Lt. Pilgrem.
Copy No. 10 to 2/Lt. Woods.
   "   " 11 " 2/Lt. A.G. Porter
   "   " 12 " H.Q. 49th I.B.
   "   " 13/14 Retained.

WAR DIARY FOR MONTH OF DECEMBER, 1916.

VOLUME 11

7th R. Inniskilling Fusiliers

Army Form C. 2118.

WAR DIARY
INTELLIGENCE SUMMARY.
(Erase heading not required.)

Place	Date	Hour	Summary of Events and Information	Remarks and references to Appendices
LOCRE	6/12/16		Batt. was relieved by the 9th R. INNIS. FUS in the Right Sub-sector & moves into Divisional Reserve at LOCRE.	
"	12/12/16		Major W.S. Rothwell hands over temp. Command to Major L.R. Farmer, 2nd R. IRISH REG. on transfer to 2nd ARMY School.	
"	12/12/16		The Batt. relieves the 9th R. INNIS FUS in the Right Sub-sector.	
"	18/12/16		The Batt. was relieved by the 9th R. INNIS FUS & moves into Brigade Reserve at KEMMEL SHELTERS.	
"	23/12/16		Major R.S. Kerr took over command from Major L.R. Farmer.	
	24/12/16		Relieves 9th R. INNIS FUS in Right Sub sector.	
	25/12/16.		Xmas Day in the Line. Quiet.	

Army Form C. 2118.

WAR DIARY
or
INTELLIGENCE SUMMARY.
(Erase heading not required.)

Place	Date	Hour	Summary of Events and Information	Remarks and references to Appendices
LOCRE	27/10/16	2.15 p.m.	Enemy trench mortars along BRIGADE FRONT & Artillery, T/M & STOKES Guns fired on him. Retaliation very weak, no casualties.	
"	30/10/16		Batt. was relieved by 1st R. INNIS. FUS. & proceeded to Brigade Reserve in KEMMEL SHELTERS.	

Major
7th R. Innis. Fus.
Comdg 30/10/16
7th R. Innis. Fus.

WAR DIARY
or
INTELLIGENCE SUMMARY.
(Erase heading not required.)

Army Form C. 2118.

Instructions regarding War Diaries and Intelligence Summaries are contained in F.S. Regs., Part II. and the Staff Manual respectively. Title pages will be prepared in manuscript.

Place	Date	Hour	Summary of Events and Information	Remarks and references to Appendices
KEMMEL SHELTERS	31/12/16	7 A.m	Major A.D. REID and Captain K.H. PARR returned from England. A battalion dinner was held at KEMMEL CHATEAU on New Years Eve.	
	1/1/17		Major A.D. REID took over command of the battalion from Major R.G. Kerr acting 2nd in Command. New Year's day – men's dinner.	
Trenches	5/1/17		Took over night out-posts from 8th Battalion :– A coy Right front line B " " " C " Left front line D " Strong points 9 & 10. Regt Street Dug-outs	
	8/1/17		Inter company relief :– "C" company relieved A coy D " " " B "	
LOCRE	9/1/17		Moved into Divisional Reserve at LOCRE (DONCASTER HUTS), bivouaced by the 8th Bn.	
Trenches	12/1/17	7.30 p.m	Small raid, 20 men of A & B coys carried out on German front line N.29.d 8.9 on the meccas, 2 prisoners, no casualties. O.C. Raid Capt Parr	
	15/1/17	8 A.m	Battalion dinner at convent LOCRE. Officers of party 2/Lt K.H. WOODS	
	17/1/17		Relieved by 8th battalion as before.	
	20/1/17		MAJOR A.D. REID granted acting rank of Lt. Colonel.	

WAR DIARY or INTELLIGENCE SUMMARY

Army Form C. 2118.

(Erase heading not required.)

Place	Date January	Hour	Summary of Events and Information	Remarks and references to Appendices
Front Line	1st	5 pm	Holding Rt. Subsector. Disposition B & C Coys Front line. A & D Support & Reserve. Batt. HQ Fort Victoria	S/S
Kemmel Shelters	5th	5/11	Battalion relieved by 7th R. Innis. Fus., & moved into Brigade Reserve Kemmel Shelters. Completion during 2 OR wounded. A considerable increase in enemy artillery activity during relief.	S/S
			Sic Brigade Reserve, Kemmel Shelters	
Kemmel Shelters			Battalion moved to Front Line, and relieved 7th. R. Innis. Fus in Right Subsector. Disposition A & B Coys Front line. B & C Coys. Support and Reserve. Battalion HQ	10/Mrs
			Sector Dickiebusch. D & A Coys Front line	
Front Line	11th		Fort Victoria.	
	12th		Enemy was Extremely active on evenings of 11th & 12th. heavily bombarding right Coy front until 7 pm	14/Mrs
			and causing much damage to our trenches	27/Mrs
	13th		C Coy relieved D Coy in Right Coy front, and on completion of relief D to be moved into Reserve.	
	15/17th		Holding Right Subsector as above	60/Mrs
	17th		Battalion relieved by 7th A. Innis. Fus, and on completion of relief moved into Divisional Reserve. Doncaster Huts Loure. Apart from enemy activity on 11th & 12th. this town was extremely quiet. Casualties. 2. OR. killed	10/Mrs
			6. OR. wounded	
			1 OR. wounded at duty	

Army Form C. 2118.

WAR DIARY
or
INTELLIGENCE SUMMARY.
(Erase heading not required.)

Instructions regarding War Diaries and Intelligence Summaries are contained in F. S. Regs., Part II. and the Staff Manual respectively. Title pages will be prepared in manuscript.

Place	Date	Hour	Summary of Events and Information	Remarks and references to Appendices
KEMMEL SHELTERS	23/1/17		Relieved by 8th Battalion and moved into Brigade Reserve KEMMEL	
	24/1/17		2/Lt I.M. MARK and 2/Lt R.C. HUGHES transferred to 36th Ulster Division	
	29/1/17		Moved into Divisional Reserve remaining at KEMMEL SHELTERS.	
	30/1/17		2/Lt R.A. HEARD went to hospital.	

31/1/17
P.J. Reid Lt Col
Comdg 7 R. Innis. Fus.

WAR DIARY.

FOR MONTH OF FEBRUARY, 1917.

VOLUME 13

UNIT :- 7th Btn R. Inniskilling Fus

WAR DIARY
or
INTELLIGENCE SUMMARY

7th (S) R. Innis. Fus.

Army Form C. 2118.

Page 4

Place	Date	Hour	Summary of Events and Information	Remarks and references to Appendices
KEMMEL SHELTERS	1/2/17		Bn. in Divisional Reserve. Route March. Lecture to officers & N.C.O's by C.O. (2/Lt. 10th R.I.F.) on the new organization of platoons.	
	4/2/17		2 Lt. J.O.L. Garry proceeded on leave to Ireland. (returned 17/2/17)	
Trenches	6/2/17		Took over the left sub sector (Spanbroek) from 6th Bn R. Ir. Regt. A + B Coys in front line C + D in Reserve. Two Coys. 4/5th R. Irish Fus. attached for tactical purposes	
	7/2/17		Capt. G.N. ROBINSON went to hospital.	
	8/2/17		Inter company relief. 'D' Coy relieved 'A' Coy in front line B " " C " " " " " 1 Platoon R. Irish Fus in S.P. 9 S.P. 11	
			2Lt. N. HAMILTON invalided to ENGLAND (sick) 23-1-17 struck off the strength accordingly (Authy Div's R.G 2097 d/31-1-17)	
			Lieut E. J. McCORMICK transferred as observer to R.F.C. Struck off the strength (Authy A.C. D/2030/2/94 d/29-1-17. D.G. Base O.R. 8174 B d/28-1-17	
			Moved into Bde. Reserve at DERRY HUTS. being relieved by 2/4 R. Innis. Fus.	
DERRY HUTS	10-2-17		2LT. C.Y. METCALFE reported for duty from England. (A/I. 10th R.I.F.)	
	11-2-17		The C.O. proceeded on C.O. Course to 2nd ARMY SCHOOL	

WAR DIARY
INTELLIGENCE SUMMARY

7th R. Innis Fus.

Army Form C. 2118.

Page 3

Place	Date 1917 Feb.	Hour	Summary of Events and Information	Remarks and references to Appendices
DERRY HUTS	12		2nd Lieut Norman BILL WOODS awarded the Military Cross for leading his Cyclist Patrol (in command) 12 Jan: 1917 from Fred St PAUL-MELL in SPANBROEK (Right & Left Sides.) inflicting many casualties in & capturing two prisoners not casualties.	
			2.4-63 S. Pte Thomas RILL awarded CROIX DE GUERRE for good work on the Somme	
	12		Lt. I.S.T. Huw Young embarked for France in the 3rd line & joining the 12th Bn with a command was; 15/2/17 Capt. A.E. Taggart " " " " " " dublin Fus: 15/2/17	
	14		2914 L/Cpl. & A/RSM. George COOMBES granted Permanent commission in 2/Lt in the R. Irish Fusiliers, 14/2/17 posted to the 7/8. R.D Irish Reg.	
	15		2/Lt. J. S. Foley appointed Actg. Adjutant. Bn: moved into Div: Reserve with Bde (DOMERTER HUTS)	
LOCRE	14		Anniversary of leaving BORDON on active service Research Gun Lionel in Dispatches. THE Bulletin.	
	16		Church & the 12 months. D-S-D 1 Commissions 2
	16		M.C 17 Promoted in 3
			Distinction
			Gran: dty wound 1
			1. dislik. disme. 37

T2134. Wt. W708-776. 500000. 4/15. Sir J. C. & S.

Army Form C. 2118.

WAR DIARY
INTELLIGENCE SUMMARY.
(Erase heading not required.) 7 R. Innis Fus?

Page 2,2,

Place	Date	Hour	Summary of Events and Information	Remarks and references to Appendices
LOIRE	Feb 1917 16		Major R.G. Kerr granted leave to Ireland 18/2/17 – 9/3/17. Lieut A.F.E. GRAVES from 6th R.I.F granted 60 B.S. on distribute unduly unaturn 27776 R.I.F	A/17757 D 7/10/15
"	17		2/Lt. R.R. Howard returned to duty from hospital.	
TRENCHES 22			Lt/F Sub Section. SPAN BRDE K.— 'A' Coy the Right Front. 'B' Coy the Left Front. 'C' " in ALBERTA DUG-OUTS. 'D' Coy in REGENT ST. DUG-OUTS. 2 Coys ('A' and 'C') 2nd Royal Irish. Regiment attached for tactical purposes. Relief completed at 5.15 P.M.— 'C' Coy relieved 'B' Coy in left front line. 'A' " " " " " " " 'D' " " " " " " "	
—	24		On relief 'B' Coy moved to ALBERTA DUG-OUTS. " A " " " " REGENT ST. DUG-OUTS. Reinforcement consisting of 4 Other Ranks arrived from the Base and were taken on the strength accordingly. 2/Lieut R.E. Poynton reported for duty on the 25th	
—	26		inst on return from	

T/134. W1. W708—776. 500000. 4/15. Sir J. C. & S.

Army Form C. 2118.

WAR DIARY

~~INTELLIGENCE SUMMARY.~~ 1st R. Inniskilling Fus. D Page 45
(Erase heading not required.)

Place	Date	Hour	Summary of Events and Information	Remarks and references to Appendices
In the Trenches	Feb 1917 26th		2 months general course of instruction at the 2nd ARMY. SCHOOL. WISQUES. Battalion relieved in the left subsection SPANBROEK by the 2nd Royal INNISKILLING. Fus. Battalion on relief went into Brigade. RESERVE. Battalion Headquarters, and 'A' and 'B' Coys to DERRY. HUTS. 'C' and 'D' Coys to the Chateau KEMMEL. Relief completed at 6.30 P.M.	
In Brigade Reserve.	27th		2/Lieut FRANCIS. DESMOND. MORPHY, 2/LIEUT. HUGH. PATRICK. HENNESSY, MONTGOMERY, and 2/LIEUT. THOMAS. JOSEPH. D'ALTON. R. IRISH REGT (Special Reserve) having reported their arrival are taken on the strength accordingly. Reinforcement consisting of 4 other ranks arrived from the Base 27.2.17 and were taken on the strength accordingly. Battalion in RESERVE at { DERRY HUTS. ('A' and 'B' Coys and Batt. H.Q's.) { KEMMEL CHATEAU ('C' and 'D' Coys).	
	28th		Operation orders received from 49th Inf. Bde. H.Q's re moving into CURRAGH CAMP DIVISIONAL RESERVE on the 2nd MARCH 1917.	Hunt-Ere Lieut Comdg 1/R. Innis Killing Fus 73

Hunt-Ere
Lieut
Comdg 1/R. Innis Killing Fus 73

WAR DIARY
FOR MONTH OF MARCH, 1917.

VOLUME 14

UNIT:- 7th Btn R. Inniskilling Fus.

Army Form C. 2118.

WAR DIARY
or
INTELLIGENCE SUMMARY
(Erase heading not required.)

5 T.R. Inniskilling Fus'r Page 46

Place	Date	Hour	Summary of Events and Information	Remarks and references to Appendices
DERRY HUTS	1/3/17		About 1.30 p.m the Germans shelled H.Qr. DERRY HUTS with 6" & 4.2" shells (about 40). Casualties 3 hence Sgt Wynn have been blown in. H.Qr Coy immediately put on their box respirators & took shelter in dug-outs. The other two Coys at DERRY HUTS occupied their appointed positions in trenches or watched H.Q. being shelled a bombing started by 2 Lieut ELVERY onto how many officers of H.Q. Coy would be left. Fortunately the betting resulted in favour of the "bookmaker". The shelling lasted about thirty minutes. An S.O.S test (gas) had been arranged for at 2 p.m. but the above shelling afforded us an opportunity of having a practical demonstration. Respirators were worn for 40 minutes.	
DERRY HUTS	2/3/17		Battalion was relieved by the 6th CONNAUGHT RANGERS, and moved at 1.30 p.m into Divisional Reserve at CURRAGH CAMP near LOCRE, on the road to WESTOUTRE.	
CURRAGH CAMP	3.3.17		Battalion in Divisional Reserve. Training carried out by company commanders. At 2 P.M all subalterns paraded in football kit for a short	

T.2134. Wt. W708—776. 500000. 4/15. Sir J. C. & S.

Army Form C. 2118.

WAR DIARY
or
INTELLIGENCE SUMMARY.
(Erase heading not required.)

Page 47

7th R. INNISKILLING Fusiliers

Place	Date	Hour	Summary of Events and Information	Remarks and references to Appendices
CURRAGH CAMP	MARCH 3rd		Cross country run. All finished except the following three who "fell out" in a state of exhaustion:- Lieut GRAVES, 2/Lieut DALTON, 2/Lieut MORPHY.	
"	4th		2/Lieut J. CUNNINGHAM reported for duty on return from sick leave England and is posted to "D" Coy. 2/Lieut W.L. McGARRY admitted Sick to 113th Field Ambulance.	
"	5th		Brigadier-General P.A. Leveson-Gower commdg 49th Inf. Bde inspected the personnel of the Transport and Quartermaster Depts. at 11 a.m. at the Transport Lines LOCRE.	
"			3 p.m. Football match. 7th Inniskillings v 7/8th R. Irish Fus: and resulted in a win for the latter by 10 points to NIL.	
"	6th		Brigade Boxing competition at the Cinema Hall. LOCRE at 2 p.m. 14314 Pte. DONOGHUE. W. "C" Coy won the Welter Weight competition.	
"	7th		The Battalion was inspected by Brig-Genl. P. Leveson-Gower 49th Inf. Bde at 10 a.m. The Battalion was drawn up in the new organization and wearing Battle Order with the exception of steel helmets. 2/Lieut. W.L. McGARRY evacuated to No 2 C.C.S. Sick.	

Army Form C. 2118.

WAR DIARY
or
INTELLIGENCE SUMMARY.

(Erase heading not required.)

Page 48

7th R. INNISKILLING Fus.

Instructions regarding War Diaries and Intelligence Summaries are contained in F. S. Regs., Part II. and the Staff Manual respectively. Title pages will be prepared in manuscript.

Place	Date	Hour	Summary of Events and Information	Remarks and references to Appendices
CURRAGH CAMP	March 8th		2/Lieut C.N.B. WALKER proceeded to ENGLAND to report at the INDIA OFFICE for personal interview and medical examination with reference to his application for permanent commission to Indian army. 2/Lieut J.T. FLANAGAN has been appointed Battalion Signalling Officer vice 2/Lieut C.N.B. WALKER	
"	9th		Brigade operation orders, re moving into the Right Subsection SPANBROEK Section received at 9.30 P.M., the battalion to move into Brigade Reserve in the 10th inst.	
"	10th		Orders to move into Brigade Reserve cancelled at 6.50 P.M. The Commdg Officer attended a conference at Bde. Headquarters at 10 a.m. 2/Lieut T.S.L. HENDERSON reported for duty on return from Sick Leave ENGLAND and was posted to 'C' Coy.	
"	11th		morning the battalion attended DIVINE SERVICES.	
"	12th		8.30 a.m. 2/Lieut S. DOLAN and 52 other ranks proceeded to be attached to the R.E. 216 Army Troops Coy.	
"	13th		Battalion in CURRAGH CAMP in Divisional Reserve, training in morning	

Army Form C. 2118.

WAR DIARY
or
INTELLIGENCE SUMMARY.
(Erase heading not required.)

Page 49

7th R. INNISKILLING Fus.

Place	Date	Hour	Summary of Events and Information	Remarks and references to Appendices
	Month			
CURRAGH CAMP	13th		Under Coy arrangements. Major R.G. KERR M.C. returned from leave and took over command of "B" Coy.	
" "	14th		A Concert was given by the "Green and Buffs" 7th R. Inniskilling Fus. Pierrot Troupe in the Cinema Hall, & were at 6 P.M. Major.Gen. W.B. HICKIE. C.B. C.M.G. D.S.O. Comdg. 16th Div. Brig.Gen. P. LEVESON-GOWER. D.S.O and Brig.Gen. A. St.Q. RICARDO. C.M.G. D.S.O. Comdg. 109th Inf. Bde. 36th Div were guests of the regiment, and after the performance dined at Battalion Headquarters mess CURRAGH CAMP. Working parties furnished for work on G.H.Q 2nd line at KEMMEL. Working from 7 a.m. to 12·30 P.M. R.S.M. DOLAN returned from ENGLAND, assumed duties of R.S.M.	
" "	16th		CAPTAIN J.W. ROBINSON happened to England Sick on 5th March 1917, and is struck off the strength of the unit accordingly Brigade operation orders re relieving the 4.8th INF. BDE in the VIERSTRAAT Section received at 10.5 P.M.	
" "	17		Battalion operation orders re relieving the 8th R. DUBLIN. Fus. in Brigade Support at BUTTERFLY FARM. VIERSTRAAT Section were issued at 5·30 P.M. The battalion pipers played the Reveille at Officers Quarters.	

Place	Date	Hour	Summary of Events and Information	Remarks and references to Appendices
CURRAGH CAMP.	MARCH 17th		Battalion attended Divine Services in the morning. On account of being ST PATRICK's day, no training was done. At 12 noon, a battalion cross country run took place. Each company entering 40 men, and Headquarters Coy 30. A very keen race resulting in a win for 'B' Coy. The first three men being :- (1) 28142. PTE. SWEENEY. M. ---- 'B' Coy. (2) 24895. " HERBERT. J ---- "A" (3) 13098 Sergt. CUNNINGHAM. T. ---- Hdqrs Coy. After dinners a football match was played :- OFFICERS. Versus. SERGEANTS. (association with a Rugger Ball). Resulted in an easy win for the officers, Score being 7 goals to NIL. At 6 P.M each Coy. held a company concert, at this free cigarettes and beer were given to the troops. Operation Orders re move to Bde. SUPPORT issued at 5-30 P.M. Battalion attended Divine Service in the morning.	
" "	18th		2/LIEUT. VICTOR. STEWART. SWYNNE having reported for duty is taken on the strength of the Battalion and posted to "C" Coy.	

Army Form C. 2118.

WAR DIARY
or
INTELLIGENCE SUMMARY.
(Erase heading not required.)

Page 57
7th R. INNISKILLING Fus.

Place	Date	Hour	Summary of Events and Information	Remarks and references to Appendices
CURRAGH CAMP	MARCH 18th		The C.O. congratulates the following Officers and Other Ranks on being honoured by the award of the IRISH BRIGADE Parchment Certificate for their "gallant conduct and constant Devotion to duty in the Field in 1916." 2/LIEUT C.N.B. WALKER. " H.P. McKENNA. 13445 A/C.S.M. G.DUNN. 3230 Sergt. A. CONWAY. 4320 Sergt. J. McCORMICK. 28665 Corpl. J. GLACKIN. 9050 Sergt. W. WALDEN. 7560 Sergt. R. GILLANDERS. 26459 Corpl. J. MAYNES. 26420. 2/Cpl. W. FAIRLESS. 24027 L/Cpl. M. FIVEY. 3306. L/Corpl. J. McCARTHY. 27576 L/Cpl. J. BROWN. 28686. L/Cpl. J. McHALE. 26501 Pte. N. BARRY. 27068 Pte W CONNOLLY. 28412 Pte M. SWEENEY. 22777. Pte. P. KELLY. 23280 " G. MAGUIRE. 24635 " T. RICE.	
" "	19th		Battalion relieved the 8th Royal DUBLIN Fusiliers in Bde Reserve at BUTTERFLY FARM. Relief completed at 12-45 a.m.	
BUTTERFLY FARM.	20th		Officers they worked the front line left sub section VIERSTRAAT SECTION. Working parties furnished for repair work in front line trenches. 30169. Corporal. F. BRANCH "D" coy proceeded to 16th Div SAS School and in sheroff the establishment	

Army Form C. 2118.

WAR DIARY
or
INTELLIGENCE SUMMARY.
(Erase heading not required.)

7th R. INNISKILLING Fusiliers

Page 58

Instructions regarding War Diaries and Intelligence Summaries are contained in F.S. Regs., Part II. and the Staff Manual respectively. Title pages will be prepared in manuscript.

Place	Date	Hour	Summary of Events and Information	Remarks and references to Appendices
BUTTERFLY FARM	MARCH 20th		CAPTAIN A. L'E. BROWNLOW, wounded 18th MAY 1916, evacuated to ENGLAND 9th June 1916, since attached 3rd Batt. R. INNIS. Fus. and.	on My M.S. to G. in C. No 9510 d/ 16-3-17
" "			LIEUT T. OLPHERT, admitted Hospital (Sick) MAY 1916 evacuated to ENGLAND 14th JUNE 1916, since attached 3rd R. INNIS. Fus. are struck off the establishment of this unit with effect from 3rd Feb 1917	authy War Office letter M.S.K d/ 15-3-17
" "	21st		Battalion in Brigade Reserve, furnishing working parties.	
" "	22nd		In Brigade Reserve. Operation Order received at 2·45 a.m from 49th Inf. Bde re relieving 8th R. INNIS. Fus'rs in front line on the 23rd March. Furnishing working parties. Battalion Operation Order re relief over front line from 8th R. INNIS Fus'rs on 23rd issued at 8·45 P.M.	
" "	23rd		In Brigade Reserve, furnishing working parties until 1 P.M. The Battalion relieved the 8th R. INNIS Fus'rs in front line left out section VIERSTRAAT Section, extending from LARK LANE exclusive to VIERSTRAAT ROAD inclusive on the left. Companies moved off from BUTTERFLY FARM at 5·30 P.M. and relief was completed at 9·30 P.M.	

T.134. Wt. W708-776. 500000. 4/15. Sir J.C. & S.

Army Form C. 2118.

WAR DIARY
or
INTELLIGENCE SUMMARY.
(Erase heading not required.)

Page 59.
7th R. INNISKILLING FUS.

Place	Date	Hour	Summary of Events and Information	Remarks and references to Appendices
	MARCH			
Front Line Trenches.	23rd		Disposition of Battalion on completion of relief was as follows:- Headquarters YORK HOUSE. (Map Reference Map Sheet WYTSCHAETE 28 S.W.2 Edition 3.E. at N.15.C.9.3.)	
VIERSTRAAT SECTOR.			'A' Coy holding night position from LARK LANE inclusive to CROWBAR TRENCH exclusive.	
			'B' " " left " " CROWBAR TRENCH inclusive to VIERSTRAAT ROAD inclusive.	
			'C' " " S.P. 13 and VAN KEEP.	
			'D' " " WATLING STREET.	
	24th		Situation Normal. 2/Lieut. ELVERY proceeded to LE TOUQUET on course of Instruction on LEWIS GUNS Disposition of Coys altered at 7 P.M. as follows. H.Q's and 1 platoon 'A' Coy withdrawn from front line to VAN KEEP. The two remaining platoons of 'A' Coy passed under the tactical orders of O.C. 'B' Coy.	
" "	25th		2/Lieuts. G.W. FAWKES and V.S. GWYNNE proceeded for course of Instruction at 16th Div School. Reinforcement of 4 men arrived from 16th I.B.D and are taken on the strength accordingly.	

Army Form C. 2118.

WAR DIARY
or
~~INTELLIGENCE~~ SUMMARY.
(Erase heading not required.)

Page 60.
7th R. INNISKILLING FUS.

Place	Date	Hour	Summary of Events and Information	Remarks and references to Appendices
In the Trenches	March 25th		The undermentioned officer is authorised to wear the Badges of R.W.R. stated against his name under Sect III of C.D.S. 584.a. CAPTAIN A.A. SEWARD. (authy 16 DIVN Nº A1(161) DIV.R.O. 2564 d. 23.3.17.	
" "	26th		Situation Normal. Intr. Coy. relief D.Coy relief 'B' Coy and 'C' Coy relief 'A'. Relief commenced at 7 p.m. complete at 9.45 p.m.	
In Bde. Support	29th		The Bn. was relieved by the 8th Rl. INNIS. FUS. in the left subsection of the VIERSTRAAT Section & moved into Bde. SUPPORT. whilst in SUPPORT Bn. was disposed as follow:— Bn. H.Qr. ROSSIGNOL FARM H.Qr. A Coy DOCTORS HOUSE 2 Platoons " LA POLKA 1 " FORT HALIFAX 1 " MOUNT ROYAL H.Qr. & 2 platoons 'B' Coy ROSSIGNOL FARM 2 " SANDBAG VILLA H.Qr. 'C' Coy DOCTORS HOUSE 4 platoons " LA POLKA	

Army Form C. 2118.

PAGE 61.

WAR DIARY
or
INTELLIGENCE SUMMARY.

7 R. INNISKILLING FUS.

(Erase heading not required.)

Place	Date	Hour	Summary of Events and Information	Remarks and references to Appendices
	March			
Bn.Bde. Support	29th 30th 31st		D.Coy SIEGE FARM. Battalion in support. Operation Orders re moving to CLARE CAMP (France Sheet 28 S.W. Edition 4 A.[M27c.3.4). issued at 12 noon.	

[signature] Lieut-Col.
Commds 7th R. Inniskilling Fus.

WAR DIARY FOR MONTH OF APRIL, 1917.

VOLUME:- 15

UNIT:- 7th R. Inniskilling Fus.

Army Form C. 2118.

WAR DIARY
or
INTELLIGENCE SUMMARY.

7th R. INNISKILLING Fusr Page 62

(Erase heading not required.)

Place	Date	Hour	Summary of Events and Information	Remarks and references to Appendices
ROSSIGNOL HOUSE	APRIL 1st		The Battalion relieved from BRIGADE SUPPORT by the 7th LEINSTER REGIMENT. Relief completed at 1 P.M. Battalion went into DIVISIONAL RESERVE LOCRE AREA.	
CLARE CAMP	2nd		to CLARE CAMP (map Ref France Sheet 28.S.W. 6d 4A. M 27 83.4.) Reinforcement of 9 other ranks arrived and were taken on the strength	
	3rd		of the Battalion accordingly. Company training being carried out. Battalion doing training. 2/LIEUT N H WOOD M.C. and 2/LIEUT H.E. LINDE reported for duty and went to be on the strength of the battalion accordingly. Reinforcement of 18 other ranks taken on the strength of the battalion.	
	4th		The following Officers were appointed 2nd in command of Coys as shown against their names :- 2/Lieut W.T. SMYTH --- 'A' Coy A/Lieut T H SHAW --- 'B' " LIEUT A.F.C. GRAVES --- 'C' " 2/LIEUT J CUNNINGHAM --- 'D' "	
	5th		Coy training being carried out. Major R.G. KER M.C. proceeded to	

Army Form C. 2118.

WAR DIARY
or
INTELLIGENCE SUMMARY.   7TH R. INNISKILLING. FUS

Page 63.

Place	Date	Hour	Summary of Events and Information	Remarks and references to Appendices
	APRIL			
CLARE CAMP	5th		ENGLAND to attend a Commd'g Officers course of Instruction at ALDERSHOT School.	
"	6th		Coy training carried out.	
"	7th		The battalion moved from CLARE CAMP to BIRR BARRACKS LUCRE. Move commenced at 4 P.M. move completed at 6.30 P.M.	
BIRR BARRACKS	8th		Fatigue parties furnished by the battalion.	
			2/LIEUT H.V. LOWRY proceeded to the 85th Grenade course at the 2nd ARMY SCHOOL, TERDEGHEM. Reinforcement consisting of 8 other ranks arrived and were taken on the strength of the battalion accordingly.	
			2/LIEUT C.N.B WALKER reported on completion of internment at INDIA Office, LONDON, which he had proceeded with reference to a permanent commission. I. A. Battalion furnishing working parties.	
	9th to 12th		On the 11th APRIL. 1917, a reinforcement of 6 other ranks arrived and were taken on the strength of the battalion accordingly.	
"	13th		The battalion less 'B' and 'C' coys which were left behind for fatigue parties moved to the RECQUES Training area by route march.	

Army Form C. 2118.

WAR DIARY
or
INTELLIGENCE SUMMARY. — 7th R INNISKILLING Fus.
Page 64

(Erase heading not required.)

Place	Date	Hour	Summary of Events and Information	Remarks and references to Appendices
On the March	APRIL 13th		The battalion paraded at 8.35 a.m. and moved off with the head of the battalion passed the ROAD JUNCTION M.29.a.35.9 Sheet 28 S.W. France. Ed. 5A. The march on the 13th was to the HAZEBROUCK area wearing:— Map Reference:— BAILLEUL Sheet: BELGIUM. HAZEBROUCK 5A STADZEELE and PRADELLES. Scale 1/100,000. The battalion halted for dinner where its head reached MOOLENACKER (1 mile S.W of METEREN) in the night. Battalion reached its billets at LA H^{te} LOGE (1 mile W of HAZEBROUCK) at 3.15 P.M. Battalion billeted at LA H^{te} LOGE for the night 13/14th APRIL. Weather fine. Distance of march about 13¾ miles.	
" "	14th		The battalion continued its march to the RECQUES area, billeting for the night 14/15th in the ST. OMER AREA. The head of the Battalion passed the road junction immediately S of the Gnst L in LA H^{te} LOGE at 8.35 a.m. (Map Reference. Sheet BELGIUM. HAZEBROUCK 5A 1/100,000).	

Army Form C. 2118.

WAR DIARY
or
INTELLIGENCE SUMMARY. 7 R. INNISKILLING FUS'S Page 65
(Erase heading not required.)

Place	Date	Hour	Summary of Events and Information	Remarks and references to Appendices
On the March	14th APRIL		The march continued via ST. OMER and was very	
			EBBLINGHEM.	Map Ref. Sheet BELGIUM HAZEBROUCK 5A.
			RENESCURE.	
			ARQUES and thence to WIZERNES	Scale 1/100,000.
			The battalion halted at 11:50 a.m. for an hour. Teas were served on the march. The battalion reached its billeting area by the night 14/15th	
			WIZERNES (about 4 miles S.W. of ARQUES) at 3:30 P.M. Weather during the march was cool and fine. Distance of march 15 miles.	
	15th "		The battalion continued its march to the RECQUES training area billeting on the night 15th APRIL and following nights at ZOUAFQUES (about 1 mile W of NORDAUSQUES (Sheet BELGIUM HAZEBROUCK 5A 1/100,000). Weather during the march was wet. The head of the battalion passed the road junction in SANDARDENNE at 9:45 a.m. The march on the 15th went to ZOUAFQUES via the :-	
			ST. MARTIN-AU-LAERT.	Map Ref. Sheet BELGIUM HAZEBROUCK 5A 1/100,000
			TILQUES.	

WAR DIARY
INTELLIGENCE SUMMARY

7R R. INNISKILLING. Fus. Page 86

Place	Date	Hour	Summary of Events and Information	Remarks and references to Appendices
On the march	15th April		MOULLE NORDAUSQUES (and thence to ZOUAFQUES) HAZEBROUCK S.A. 1/100,000 } Sheet BELGIUM The battalion halted for an hour at 12 noon. Teas were served on the march at 12 noon near MOULLE. The battalion arrived in billets at ZOUAFQUES at 3-45 P.M. Today's march was about 14 miles. 'B' and 'C' Coys left behind in BIRR BARRACKS LOCRE (Map Ref Sheet Belgium 28.S.W. Ed SA 1/20,000) M 23 c.7.6 travelled by motor lorry and rejoined the battalion in billets at ZOUAFQUES. Distance marched on the three days 13th, 14th and 15th APRIL was 43 miles.	
ZOUAFQUES	16th April		Platoon training carried out. The battalion marched out from billets to the training area, and then split up into companies for training purposes. Training from 9 a.m. to 1-30 p.m. Afternoon games, and rest for the men. Reinforcement of 24 other ranks arrived and were taken up the strength of the battalion accordingly.	
" "	17th "		Platoon Training being carried out. 2/Lieut. J.T. FLANAGAN and 6 other	

Army Form C. 2118.

WAR DIARY
or
INTELLIGENCE SUMMARY. 7H. R. INNISKILLING. FUS. Force G7.

(Erase heading not required.)

Place	Date	Hour	Summary of Events and Information	Remarks and references to Appendices
ZOUAFQUES	APRIL 17th		Runners proceeded to be attached to the 49th Infy. Bde. Signal Section in accordance with instructions upon Inf. Bde. No S.S. 2/11 d 16.4.17 & R14 & d 17.4.17	d 17.4.17
"	18th		2/LIEUT C.N.B. WALKER resumes his duties as Signalling Officer to the Battalion with effect from to-day's date.	
			A/Lieut. T.H. SHAW granted special leave to ENGLAND until 30th APRIL 1917.	
			2/LIEUT. R.A. HEARD is appointed Intelligence Officer to the Battalion in addition to his duties as Hdqr. Lewis Gun Detachment.	
"	19th	"	Day training carried out in the arrangements made by Company commrs. Rearrangement of Tattoo numbers arrived and are taken on the Strength of the Battalion accordingly.	
"	20th	"	Battalion marched off at 8 A.M. for Musketry Training on Range "B" 2nd Army Musketry School near MOULLE (Sheet HAZEBROUCK 5A 1/10000) ROUTE to Range being via NORDAUSQUES and MONNÉCOVE.	
"	22nd		Church Parades and & rest for the men.	

WAR DIARY or INTELLIGENCE SUMMARY

7H R. INNISKILLING FUS

Army Form C. 2118.
Page 68.

Place	Date	Hour	Summary of Events and Information	Remarks and references to Appendices
ZOUAFQUES	APRIL 21st		Coy training under coy arrangements. Afternoon 3rd Round of Brigade championship football played:— "SOCCER" 7H INNISKILLINGS — 10 goals Bde. H.Q.'s and T.M. Battery — NIL "RUGGER" 7H INNISKILLINGS — 9 points 2nd R. IRISH REGT. — NIL	
"	22nd		2/LIEUT H.P. MONTGOMERY is appointed Battalion Signalling Officer vice 2/LIEUT C.N.B. WALKER to duty and posted to 'B' Coy.	
"	23rd		Battalion marched off at 8 a.m. for musketry training at 'B' Range and during musketry school. Tests were carried on the ranges, and dinners on return to Billets. Demonstration effect of Lewis gun fire and companies firing on the move covered by Rifle Grenade fire. Brigade dromest at ammn shed this day.	
"	24th		In the two trenchy Runs 3618 Corporal Smith F. 'B' coy was the first	

WAR DIARY
INTELLIGENCE SUMMARY

(Erase heading not required.)

7th R. INNISKILLING. Fus. Page 69.

Army Form C. 2118.

Place	Date	Hour	Summary of Events and Information	Remarks and references to Appendices
ZOUAFQUES	APRIL 24th		Manœuvres. In the Bomb Throwing competition this battalion was 2nd being beaten by 1 point by the 2nd R. IRISH REGT.	
			2nd in the Reckoning Drill competition	
			2nd " Rehearsing Beatings "	
			2nd " Wiring " "	
			2nd " Wounded " "	
"	25th		The battalion marched off at 8.15 a.m. to the training area for a battalion training. Afternoon HOCKEY MATCH against 2nd R. Ir. Regt, resulting in a draw.	
"	26th		2/Lieut O'BRIEN proceeded to ABBEVILLE to a course of Instruction in Transport Duties. Brigade attack scheme carried out in the 26th inst, wherof of Hoeb v WYTSCHAETE ridge afternoon Replayed Semi final Brigade football championship 7th INNISKILLINGS 2 goals 1 goal (after 20 minutes extra time) 8th " " "	
"	27th		Battalion training in the new formations. To-day being the anniversary of the Gas attack at ST JULIEN the	

Army Form C. 2118.

WAR DIARY
or
INTELLIGENCE SUMMARY.
(Erase heading not required.) 7th R. INNISKILLING. Fus. Page 70

Place	Date	Hour	Summary of Events and Information	Remarks and references to Appendices
ZOUAFQUES	APRIL 27th		Greeting letter was received by the Commdg. Officer from Maj. General HICKIE. C.B. commanding the Division:— "I wish you please convey to all officers and men of the Battalion under your command my good wishes to them on this the first anniversary of the defeat of the BAVARIAN attack at HULLUCH. On that occasion the 7th BATTALION nobly kept up the traditions of the Royal INNISKILLING. Fus. I take this opportunity of expressing to all ranks my appreciation of the present Spirit and smartness of the Battalion. Extract from Battalion Routine Orders dated 27.4.17. "I am extremely confident that one and all intend to maintain the honour of your Battalion and the glorious traditions of your Regiment, as you did so nobly a year ago. You have shown this spirit on every subsequent opportunity and you will, I know, continue to do so in the future." (Sd) H.N.Y. Lt.Col. 27.4.17	

WAR DIARY
INTELLIGENCE SUMMARY.
7th R. INNISKILLING. Fus. Page 71

Place	Date	Hour	Summary of Events and Information	Remarks and references to Appendices
ZOUAFQUES	APRIL 27th		Brigade Championship Football Finals played in the afternoon:—	
			"SOCCER FINAL"	
			2nd R. IRISH REGT — 1 goal	
			7th R. INNISKILLING Fus — NIL	
			"RUGGER FINAL"	
			7/8th R. IRISH FUS — 9 points	
			7th R. INNIS. Fus — NIL	
			2/Lieut J.V.L. McGARRY admitted to 113th Field Ambulance 4.3.17, evacuated sick to No 2 CCS 6-3-17, rejoined the battalion on the 27th April and is posted to "D" Coy.	
			The battalion started its march from the BECQUES bivouac area	
"	28th		The battalion paraded and moved off so that its head passed the end of ZOUAFQUE'S village moving towards NORDAUSQUES at 9.50 a.m.	
			The march on the 28th was to WIZERNES area:—	

Army Form C. 2118.

WAR DIARY
or
INTELLIGENCE SUMMARY.
(Erase heading not required.)

7th R. INNISKILLING FUS. Page 72

Instructions regarding War Diaries and Intelligence Summaries are contained in F. S. Regs., Part II. and the Staff Manual respectively. Title pages will be prepared in manuscript.

Place	Date	Hour	Summary of Events and Information	Remarks and references to Appendices
On the march	APRIL 28th		MOULLE } Map Ref. Sheet ST MARTIN-AU-LAERT } BELGIUM. HAZEBROUCK S.A. 1/100000). Bivouac for the night in WIZERNES. A one hour's halt was made at 12.50 P.M. Teas were served on the march. The battalion reached billets at 3.35 P.M. Distance of march about 14 miles.	
"	29th		The battalion entrained its march bLUCRE, and it had of the battalion pleasing the road junction S of S in WIZERNES at 8.40 a.m. and marched via WESTCOVE through ARQUES, & thence to LA THÉ LOGE. A one hour halt was made at 12 noon. Teas were served in the march. The battalion arrived in billets for the night at LA HTE LOGE at 3.35 P.M. (immediately W of HAZEBROUCK). Distance about 15 miles.	
"	30th		The battalion completed its march to LUCRE. The head of the battalion	

Army Form C. 2118.

WAR DIARY
or
INTELLIGENCE SUMMARY.
(Erase heading not required.)

7th R. INNISKILLING Fus. Page 73

Place	Date	Hour	Summary of Events and Information	Remarks and references to Appendices
On the march	April 30		will pass the first cross Roads from LA H^{TE} LOGE towards HAZEBROUCK at 7-25 a.m. march to be one	
			BAILLEUL and thence to LOCRE	
			The IX corps commander inspected the Battalion near [post?] at 11-57 a.m., as it marched through BAILLEUL.	
			The battalion reached LOCRE at 1-15 p.m. and halted for a 3½ hours halt at LOCRE when dinners were served. at 4.45 P.M battalion marched to CARNAVON CAMP (Map Ref. Sheet France 28 S.W. M10 6·5·9)	
			During the 6 days march 13th 14, 15th, 28, 29th and 30th APRIL 1917. only one man fell out and he had the medical Officers permission, but a single man quitted the ranks during the 6 days march, nor was assisted by the Transport or otherwise, except within the day, i.e riding the toy [transcho?] horses etc.	
			Average strength of the battalion was roughly 30 Officers and 670 other ranks, 55 horses and usual transport.	

H. W. [?] Lt Col
[?] 7th [?]

W A R   D I A R Y :
-------------oOo----------

VOLUME:- 16

FOR MONTH OF MAY, 1917.

UNIT:- 7th Royal Inniskilling Fus.

Army Form C. 2118.

WAR DIARY
or
INTELLIGENCE SUMMARY.
(Erase heading not required.)

7/8(S) B" R INNISKILLING FUS Page 74

May 1917

Place	Date	Hour	Summary of Events and Information	Remarks and references to Appendices
MURRUM= BRIDGE CAMP	May 1st		The Bⁿ in Brigade Reserve to the Brigade which moved into the DIEPENDAAL Sector on the night 1/2 May	
DITTO				
RENINGHELST -LA CLYTTE Road	2nd		ditto	
	3rd		"	
	4th		A draft of 15 men arrived, of whom 5 originally belonging to the 8th Bⁿ were posted there	
	5th		On the night of the 5/6th May. The Bⁿ relieved the 8th Bⁿ R. Innis Fus." in the right sub Sector of the DIEPENDAAL Sector	
DIEPENDAAL Right Sub Section	6th		In the DIEPENDAAL Sector	
	7th		Captain. W. H. COLLIS reported for duty 6/5/17 & is posted to D. Coy	
"	8th		DIEPENDAAL Sector	
"			draft of 5 men with 7th Fusrds arrived	
"	9th		Relieved by 7th Bⁿ E. Lanc. Regt. 56 NCOs & 19 O.Rs on night of 9/10 May and moved into DE ZON CAMP on the LA CLYTTE-LOCRE Road via 3. G. 5.	
		9.15PM	The relief was timed to commence at 10 P.M. at 9:15 P.M. the enemy opened an intense bombardment along the whole front and nearer lines 17/12	

Army Form C. 2118.

WAR DIARY
or
INTELLIGENCE SUMMARY

7/E R. INNIS FUS;

(Erase heading not required.)

Pages 75

Place	Date	Hour	Summary of Events and Information	Remarks and references to Appendices
DIEPENDAAL Right Sub-Section	May 9th	9.15PM	This sub-section, the area bombardment continuing in to the 7/7th Sub-Section relief the 7/E R. Irish Fus= Poppy Lane. (The communication trench on the right of the Right sub-section was approximately the 7/7th. It has been bombarded, it received two direct hits from 5.9". The Germans used 5.9"s and 4.2"s on what is known as the new Reserve Trench, which was occupied by "B" & "D" No 7Platoons (Hq's & 1 Platoon A C" (2/Lt Smithson) on the right "B" C" (Lieut Trimble) in the centre D C" (Capt Stainforth) also 1 Platoon (2.Lt Cunningham), which was on the 7/7th front line, on the 7/7L & "C" "(A/Capt" Seward) was on the right in the front line, the remainder of 9 Platoons 7A C" were in reserve portions of the front occupied by the 13". The Germans used Shrapnel generously on the front line, their shooting generally speaking was good, but nothing exceptional. The 7/7th & the new Reserve line had the worst time. 7A B" L/S Capt W.H. Collis, killed and 3 O.R's killed and 10 O.Rs	

WAR DIARY
or
INTELLIGENCE SUMMARY

Army Form C. 2118.

Page 76

7th R. Innis: Fusiliers

May 1917

Place	Date	Hour	Summary of Events and Information	Remarks and references to Appendices
"	May 9th		wounded. D Coy HQ's & Telephone Office was destroyed almost immediately and communication by him was never reestablished. B Coy comm. was twice cut and mended. (B Coy had 1 man wounded) There was no scheme of an attack by the Germans who were apparently to evacuate their own front line and subject actually fired their own T/M's into it and after the bombardment which communication trenches back to their front & support lines.	
		10.15pm	lasted exactly an hour, were found bombing their way down their Our own artillery were extraordinarily quick in opening fire and kept up a heavy fire from within a few minutes of the Germans opening fire until when their own M/G's however opened There was no rifle fire on either side on the German front. a burning c along the German front. The runner 17 Capt. Stein Joseph P.S. (this & 2nd Dunn D. Coy were b/[wounded] brought to the notice of the Bn Comm. & 5 NCO R & m for their with [illegible]	

Army Form C. 2118.

WAR DIARY
or
INTELLIGENCE SUMMARY.
(Erase heading not required.)

7th R. Innis. Fus.   Page 77

Place	Date	Hour	Summary of Events and Information	Remarks and references to Appendices
"	May 9th		conduct.	
DE ZON CAMP Nr LA CLYTTE DOURE Rd	10th	2 AM	The Bn. arrived in this camp about 2 AM	
Support Rs in VIERSTRAAT SECTOR	10th	12.15 PM	The Bn. moved out to take over duties of support Bn. on the 49th Inf. Bde. moving into the line in the VIERSTRAAT SECTION and took over from the 7th Leinster Regt. (ToT STANLEY) STANDS	
"		9 PM	In the evening Capt. W. H. DOUGLAS, 24681 Pte. H. BUTT, 19688 Pte. H. HIGGINS ON 40297 Pte. F. REYNOLDS of 118th DIV were buried in the LA LAITRIE cemetery on the VIERSTRAAT-KEMMEL RIDGE (These men were killed on the 9th inst.). A draft of 23 men arrived from FERMOY 10 + 5 men were sent over from the 8th Bn. who had arrived in a draft for them and who originally belonged to this Bn.	
"	10th		Capt: STAINFORTH recommended for ribbon in STHORPOY message for ribbons during bombardment of the 9th May. 20863 Pte. E. CHISHOLM D.C.M. recommended	

T2134. Wt. W708—776. 500000. 4/15. Sir J. C. & S.

Army Form C. 2118.

WAR DIARY
or
INTELLIGENCE SUMMARY.
(Erase heading not required.)

2 R. Irish Fus.   May 1917   Page 75

Place	Date	Hour	Summary of Events and Information	Remarks and references to Appendices
	May 11		9pr Croix de Guerre for wishes and conveys in attempting to the wounded in the festive front of the New Reserve Trench during the bombardment of the 9th J.P. May. BJSK recommendations phoned through to Brigade in answer to their SEC/B B&4 11 May 1917.	
SUPPORT. VIERSTRAAT Section.	12		Battalion in support in the VIERSTRAAT SECTOR. Working parties being furnished. A draft of 15th other ranks arrived from the 16th Inf. Base Depot and were taken on the strength of the battalion accordingly.	
	13		49th Inf. Bde. Order No. 12 d. 12.5.17, re relieving the 2nd R. Irish Regt in the Right Front line VIERSTRAAT SECTOR received at 10.40 a.m. Batt. Operation Order No. 35 d. 13.5.17, re relieving 2nd R. Irish Regt issued at 2-45 p.m. Working parties being furnished.	
	14.		The battalion at an noted above commenced at 3 P.M. and was completed at 5-10 P.M. Situation on front normal.	
FRONT LINE	15	3.P.M.	Situation on front normal. Trench mortar bombardment on PETIT BOIS commenced at 3 P.M. carried by 8" and 6" Howitzer batteries. Enemy's retaliation very feeble. LIEUT- COL. YOUNG N.G. D.S.O very slightly wounded whilst looking in the Sun outside Batt. H.Q'rs. The wounds being caused by a piece	

Army Form C. 2118.

WAR DIARY
or
INTELLIGENCE SUMMARY.
(Erase heading not required.)

7th R. INNISKILLINGS Fus. Page 79

Place	Date	Hour	Summary of Events and Information	Remarks and references to Appendices
Front Line	May 15		O/H.E. wounds being on right arm. 2/Lieuts. G. HENDERSON and METCALFE returned from a 5 days Platoon Commrs course held at the Brigade School. 2/Lieut. D.V.L. McGARRY being reported to 7/8th R. IRISH FUS, is ordered off the strength of the battalion accordingly to report to 7/8th R. IRISH FUS. 2/Lieut. S. DICKSON transferred from C. Coy to "B" Coy.	Authy:- A/50 A/1757 dt 30.4.17 47/1B SCC IV/319 21/4. 3.15.
" "	16th		2/LIEUTS W.T. SMYTH and 2/LIEUT. T.H. SHAW proceeded to a 5 days Platoon Commrs course held at the Brigade School. Situation on front normal.	
" "	17th	2.30 P.M.	Batt. Operation Orders re relief by the 8th R. DUBLIN Fus issued.	
" "	18th		Situation normal. Relief of the Battalion by the 8th R. DUBLIN Fus commenced at 3 P.M. Relief completed at 4.36 P.M. On completion of the relief the Battalion moved into BIRR BARRACKS. LOCRE.	
BIRR BARRACKS "			5717. C.S.M. GALLAGHER. 'B' Coy having been found permanently unfitted	

Army Form C. 2118.

WAR DIARY
or
INTELLIGENCE SUMMARY.
(Erase heading not required.)

7th R. INNISKILLING. FUS^{rs}   Page 80

Place	Date	Hour	Summary of Events and Information	Remarks and references to Appendices
BIR R BARRACKS	MAY 18th	—	For duties at the front proceeded to the BASE DEPOT N° 36 HAVRE. Battalion in DIVISIONAL RESERVE at LOEURE. Working parties being furnished.	Authy 16th DIV N° A/244/6 d. 13.5.17. A.D.M.S 16th DIV N° P34 d. 14.5.17.
" "	19th	—	2/Lieut H.E. LINDE 'A' Coy transferred to 'C' Coy.	
" "	20th	—	2/Lieut S.L. HENDERSON 'C' " " " 'A' " 2/Lieut D.W. HOLMES proceeded to LA LEVRETTE to attend a course of instruction in Stokes Mortar. Lieut-Col H.N. YOUNG proceeded to ENGLAND on short special leave. Reinforcement of 60 other ranks arrived from 16th I.B.D and are taken on the strength of the battalion accordingly. Working parties being furnished.	
" "	21st	—	2/Lieut J.S. FOLEY and 7 other ranks proceeded to 2nd Army Rest Camp AMBLETEUSE near BOULOGNE for a fortnight rest. Working parties being furnished.	
" "	22nd	—	Reinforcement of 14 Other Ranks arrived from 16th I.B.D are taken on the strength accordingly. 2/Lieut J.S. GWYNNE admitted to hospital on the 20.5.17. was evacuated from N° 53 C.C.S to the BASE (Authy A.D.M.S 16th DIV N° 273/90 d. 21.5.17)	

Army Form C. 2118.

WAR DIARY
or
INTELLIGENCE SUMMARY
(Erase heading not required.)

7'R. INNISKILLING Fus. Page 81

Place	Date	Hour	Summary of Events and Information	Remarks and references to Appendices
BIRR	May 23-24		Working parties furnished for work in the lines etc.	
BARRACKS	25"		2/Lieut. I.F. O'BRIEN rejoined the battalion from Transport service, and appointed to act as assistant Transport Officer. Usual working parties furnished.	
	27"		A reinforcement of 45 other ranks arrived from 16th I.B.D. and are to be on the strength of the Battalion accordingly.	
			LIEUT-COL H.N. YOUNG D.S.O returned from leave. CAPTAIN D.H. MORTON rejoined the Battalion on the 26th inst. is taken on the strength of the battalion accordingly and is posted to 'B' Coy. CAPTAIN. D.H. MORTON took over the command and Pay of 'B' Coy with effect from to-day.	
	28"			
	29th	2.A.M	At 2 a.m. gas alarm was sounded. Batt "Stood to". At 2.10 a.m. B&H "Stood down" word being received from Brigade that it was a false alarm. Transport lines were shelled and resulted in 10thranks being wounded. 2/LIEUT. WILFRED GORDON BAKER reported for duty and is taken on the strength of the Battalion accordingly.	
	30th		2/LIEUT. ALBERT HERBERT H ARMSTRONG reported for duty and is taken on the Ren	

WAR DIARY
INTELLIGENCE SUMMARY

7th R. INNISKILLING. Fus. Page 82

Place	Date	Hour	Summary of Events and Information	Remarks and references to Appendices
BIRR BARRACKS	30th May		on the strength of the Battalion accordingly and is posted to 'C' Coy for duty. LIEUT. A.F.C. GRAVES proceeded to course of instruction at 49th Bde & A/LIEUT H.V. LOWRY } School. CAPTAIN C.H. STAINFORTH and A/CAPT A.A. SEWARD proceeded to WAILLY, near ARRAS to attend a demonstration on the "use of TANKS in an attack."	
" "	31st May		Working parties being furnished.	

A.M.Lowry
Lieut-Col
Commdg 7th R. Innis Killing Fus.

WAR DIARY.

FOR MONTH OF JUNE, 1917.

VOLUME :- 17

UNIT :- 7th Battn Royal Inniskilling Fus.

Army Form C. 2118.

WAR DIARY
or
INTELLIGENCE SUMMARY.
(Erase heading not required.)

7th R INNISKILLING. June Page 33

Place	Date	Hour	Summary of Events and Information	Remarks and references to Appendices
BIRR BARRACKS LOCRE.	June 1st		Battalion in DIVISIONAL RESERVE in BIRR BARRACKS furnishing working parties. Battalion orders got the offensive together with appendices issued on the 1st inst to all concerned.	
" "	2nd		Battalion furnishing working parties. The battalion relieved the 7th R. IRISH RIFLES at BUTTERFLY FARM (Map Ref Sheet KEMMEL 28 SW1 Ed3 T0000 N19 a 7.9) Relief completed at 10.15 P.M.	
BUTTERFLY FARM	3rd		2/LIEUT. W.T. SMYTH proceeded to a course of Instruction on Bombing at the IX Corps School LA LEVRETTE on the 3rd June 1917. 2/LIEUT. S. DOLAN proceeded on the 18th May to BERTHEN (near BAILLEUL) to be employed at the DIVISIONAL Reinforcement Camp. MAJOR R.S. KERR M.C. is Struck off the strength of the Battalion with effect from 6th APRIL 1917. Authy. S.R.O 2348 of 29.5.17 2/LIEUT. J. CUNNINGHAM proceeded to LE TOUQUET on the 4th inst to attend a course of Instruction in Lewis Gun.	
" "	4th			
" "	5th		Battalion in BUTTERFLY CAMP getting equipped and ready for the offensive. Battalion relieving the 8th R. INNISKILLING Fus in the left sub section	

Army Form C. 2118.

WAR DIARY
or
~~INTELLIGENCE~~ SUMMARY.
(Erase heading not required.)

7th R. INNISKILLING Fus   Page 84

Place	Date	Hour	Summary of Events and Information	Remarks and references to Appendices
BUTTERFLY FARM	June 5		2 of the VIERSTRAAT Section. Relief to commence at 11.30 P.M. 2/Lieut A.H.H ARMSTRONG took over the duties of Asst Adjutant (temporary) with effect from 4th June vice 2/Lt C.H. HOLLIST, sent down to F. Ambce sick. 13133. Regt Sergt Major R. TOLAN wounded by Shrapnel on the 4th June. Disposition of the Battalion on the night 5/6th June 1917 was as follows:— Battalion Headquarters — THE FOSSE (VIERSTRAAT-KEMMEL Rd) 'B' Coy (Front Line) — from N18a 50.00 to where VIERSTRAAT ROAD cuts front line 'A' Coy } 'D' " } Reserve Line. (The PARK and CHINESE WALL LINE) 'C' " } VIERSTRAAT SWITCH running immediately east of VIERSTRAAT-KEMMEL Rd. T.M.O's & Lewis Gunners — Reserve Line — (CHINESE WALL LINE on the S of its junction with USNAG H. STREET. (communication runs Support & Reserve Lines). (2 Lewis Guns).	

Army Form C. 2118.

WAR DIARY
~~INTELLIGENCE~~ SUMMARY
(Erase heading not required.)

7th R. INNISKILLING Fusiliers. Page 85

Instructions regarding War Diaries and Intelligence Summaries are contained in F. S. Regs., Part II. and the Staff Manual respectively. Title pages will be prepared in manuscript.

Place	Date	Hour	Summary of Events and Information	Remarks and references to Appendices
In the line	5th June		2/Lieut. C. H. FFOLLIOTT "D" Coy evacuated to hospital with Battalion completed its equipment with rifle grenades and bombs prior to the attack.	
	6 June		Battalion Operation Order No 37 re battalion cleaning up to summary positions for the attack issued to all concerned. The following Officers were selected to go with the Battalion in the attack.	
			Headquarters:-	
			Lieut-Col. H. N. YOUNG. D.S.O. in command	
			CAPTAIN. J. H. PARR. M.C. O.C 2nd in Command	
			CAPTAIN A.C. TAGGART Adjutant	
			2/Lieut H.P.H MONTGOMERY Signalling Officer.	
			" " R. A. HEARD Intelligence Officer	
			"A" Company:-	
			2/Lieut. S. L. HENDERSON Commander.	
			" " W.M.M. ELVERY	

WAR DIARY
or
INTELLIGENCE SUMMARY.

7R INNISKILLING Fusiliers Page 96.

Army Form C. 2118.

Place	Date	Hour	Summary of Events and Information	Remarks and references to Appendices

In the Line	JUNE 6th		'A' Company (continued).
			
			  2/Lieut. H.W. RUDDOCK
			  " " R.E. POYNTON.
			
			'B' Company :-
			
			  Lieut. A.E.C. TRIMBLE. ---- Commander.
			  2/Lieut. C.N.B. WALKER.
			  " " H.R. McKENNA.
			  " " S. DICKSON
			
			'C' Company :-
			
			  Captain. A.A. SEWARD. ---- Commander.
			  2/Lieut. H.E. LINDE.
			  " " C.W. FAWKES.
			  " " F.D. MURPHY.
			
			'D' Company :-
			
			  Captain. C.H. STAINFORTH. ---- Commander.
			  2/Lieut. C.A. METCALFE.	

WAR DIARY or INTELLIGENCE SUMMARY

7. R. INNISKILLING. Fus Page 87

Place	Date	Hour	Summary of Events and Information	Remarks and references to Appendices
In the Line	6th JUNE		D Coy (continued) 2/LIEUT. W.S. BAKER. " " T.J. D'ALTON. Medical Officer -- CAPT. G.O.F. ALLEY. M.C. R.A.M.C. The battalion commenced moving up to its assembly position at 10 P.M. Assembly Positions:- Front line N18a 55.00 to VIERSTRAAT ROAD (inclusive) whence it cuts the front line Support Line. SHANNON TRENCH from N18a 35.00 to the VIERSTRAAT ROAD (inclusive). 'A' Coy in front line from N18a 55.00 to point 50 yds N of MAYO STREET. communication which 'B' " " " " 50 yds N of MAYO ST. to VIERSTRAAT ROAD. 7 runs from N18 d 7 to N18 b 1 'C' " " Support line on the right? } SHANNON TRENCH from N18a 35.00 'D' " " " " left } to the VIERSTRAAT ROAD (inclusive) Ditching line between coys in Support line being at N18 a 53.40. "Jumping up" Section supplied by 8th Royal Inniskilling Fus. (B Coy commanded by CAPTAIN. W.R. MAGUIRE.) Nº. I, II, III, IV of L Sections of the "Jumping up" assembled in the front line between N18a 55.00 and the VIERSTRAAT—WYTSCHAETE Rd. where it cuts the front line.	

WAR DIARY or INTELLIGENCE SUMMARY

Army Form C. 2118

7th ROYAL INNISKILLING FUSS Page 88

Place	Date	Hour	Summary of Events and Information	Remarks and references to Appendices
In the Line	June 6th		"Suppers up" Sections Nos VI, VII, VIII, IX, X, XI and XII arrived in the Support Line, that is SHANNON TRENCH from N18a 35.00 to the VIERSTRAAT - WYTSCHAETE ROAD (inclusive). The "Suppers up" was formed by "B" Coy 8th ROYAL INNISKILLING FUSILIERS. Captain W.R. MAGUIRE ---- Commanding 2/Lieut. NEALON ---- Nº 4 Platoon " " PATTERSON ---- " 5 " " Lieut. BROWNE ---- " 6 " " 'C' Section 49th M.G. Coy (Lieut. BELLAMY) was attached to the Battalion. The enemy's position was in SHANNON TRENCH (support trench) at its junction with USNA G.H. STREET (communication trench). Nº 2. Section 49th Trench Mortar Battery (Lieut. LEPETON) was attached to the Battalion. The enemy's position was in the T.M. Emplacement in the Brutish front line about 150 yards to the left (i.e. North) of MAYO STREET (communication line). "A" Coy 8th ROYAL INNIS. FUSS a carrying party furnished by 1 Platoon was attached to the Battalion for communication by 2/Lieut. HENDERSON was attached to the Battalion for carrying purposes. The enemy's position was on the Support Line (SHANNON TRENCH from N18a 35.00 to the VIERSTRAAT-WYTSCHAETE Rd exclusive).	

WAR DIARY or INTELLIGENCE SUMMARY

7th R. INNISKILLING Fusiliers Page 89

Army Form C. 2118

Place	Date	Hour	Summary of Events and Information	Remarks and references to Appendices
In the field	June 6th		Battalion Headquarters were in WSNAGH. STREET. (Map. Ref. WYTSCHAETE Sheet 28 S.W.2. & S.A Scale 1/10,000. N.18.d.15.45). The battalion and all other troops attached to the battalion for the attack were in position in their assembly trenches at	
"	7th	1.30 a.m.	1.35 a.m. 7th June. Battalion on the flanks of the battalion were as follows:— On the Right :— 7/8th ROYAL. IRISH. Fusiliers 16th DIVISION. (49th Inf. Bde) On the Left :— 6th Bn. THE WILTSHIRE. REGIMENT. 19th DIVISION.(58th " ") The Battalion Dump was in the immediate vicinity of the ʮ in UNNAMED. WOOD. map reference WYTSCHAETE 28 S.W.2. & S.A.(0.13 c.1.6).	
"	"	3.10 a.m.	at zero hour 3.10 a.m. immediately after the advance of men had commenced, the leading coys of the attack 'A' and 'B' companies left the trenches and advanced close up to our barrage. The attack was carried out on a two company frontage, four waves. The first and second waves were formed by 'A' and 'B' coys attacking side by side. 'A' coy on the right and 'B' coy on the left. The third and fourth waves were formed by 'C' and 'D' coys. 'C' coy attacking side by side. 'C' coy on the right of 'D' coy.	

Army Form C. 2118

WAR DIARY or INTELLIGENCE SUMMARY

(Erase heading not required.)

7th R. INNISKILLING. Fus. Page 90

Place	Date	Hour	Summary of Events and Information	Remarks and references to Appendices
In the line	June 7	—	The Second wave left our front line about 100 yards behind the first wave. There were no counter attacks and enemy's front and support trenches were much deserted. On reaching the first objective, NAIL SWITCH, m/o R.I. Sheet 28 S.W.2. WYTSCHAETE. N18 b 6.4 to 18 c 5.7, no head of a man could be found, and the platoons detailed for the attack moved on to the 2nd objective, the RED CHATEAU LINE, that is from N18 b 8.2 to N18 d 6.6. Sheet WYTSCHAETE 28 S.W.2. This on the night of 7th/8th pushed patrols forward about twelve meters from where the enemy, who had established themselves in shell holes, were immediately dealt with. The O.C. 'A' Coy (2/Lieut H.W. RUDDOCK) moved his joint went up to the RED LINE (O13 c 15.60 — O13 c 3.8. Sheet WYTSCHAETE 6 W.2.) on the RED CHATEAU LINE was not a good one either from the point of view of a line of defence or from which to consolidate on account of the shelling from our own guns, then proceeded with at 5-12 a.m. and joined up with the 7/8th R. IRISH Fus on the right. The O.C. is my own 'B' Coy (LIEUT A.E.C. TRIMBLE) and informed him of the disposition of 'A' Coy, then advanced and confirmed with using 'A' Coy, wrong the RED LINE from O13 c 15.60 — O13 c 2.18 and 'D' Coys, forming the line temporarily that is	

WAR DIARY
INTELLIGENCE SUMMARY

Army Form C. 2118

7th R. INNISKILLING FUS. Page 9

Place	Date	Hour	Summary of Events and Information	Remarks and references to Appendices
In the Line	7 June		third and fourth waves of the attack passed through "A" and "B" Coys to take the Battalion 3rd Objective, THE RED LINE, Map Reference Sheet 28 SW2. WYTSCHAETE. O13c.15.60 to O13c.2.8. and to take and consolidate the Batt. Fourth (final Objective) the BLUE LINE. Map Reference Sheet 28 SW2 WYTSCHAETE O13c.8.12 to O13c.9.7. A certain amount of opposition was experienced on the RED and BLUE LINES, though nothing of a really serious nature. A few machine guns fired on our advance but no enemy opposition was put up by the enemy. The BLUE LINE was reached by "C" and "D" Coys at 4.45 a.m. in touch with 7/8th R. IRISH Fus. on the right, and in touch with WELSH REGT. (19th DIV) on the left. A battalion of the T.M. Battery under LIEUT. LEPETON attached to the section of the SUNKEN ROAD wired the BLUE the Batt. had up a position to employ them. LINE, but their was no occasion to employ them. After the capture of the BLUE LINE. The Battalion Helgo moved forward at 5.32 a.m. to advance Battalion Helgo at UNNAMED WOOD Sheet 28 SW2 WYTSCHAETE O13c.1.5. Consolidation of the BLUE LINE commenced. The 2nd R. IRISH REGIMENT passed through the BLUE LINE	

WAR DIARY or INTELLIGENCE SUMMARY

7th R. INNISKILLING Fus. Page 92.

Army Form C. 2118

Place	Date	Hour	Summary of Events and Information	Remarks and references to Appendices
In the Line	7 June		At 6.50 a.m. the O.C. 'B' Coy furnished a platoon to hold and garrison a strong point in vicinity of O13c 15.90 (RED POST). This platoon moved to strong point and is temporarily by the R.E. It was occupied at 5 P.M. The following were the hours on which columns for the eximent and departure from the various coloured times:—	
			Zero hour 3.10 a.m.	
			RED LINE { arrive 0.35 / Depart 1.05.	
			BLUE LINE { arrive 1.40 / Depart 3.40	
			The Battalion Objectives were:—	
			1st Objective --- --- NAIL SWITCH N18 b.6.4 to N18c 5.7	
			2nd " --- --- RED CHATEAU LINE N18 b 8.2 to N18 d.6.5 including the RED CHATEAU at N18 d 8.9	
			3rd " --- --- RED LINE O13c 15.60 to O13c 2.8	
			4th " --- --- BLUE LINE O13c 8.2 to O13c 9.7.	
			'A' and 'B' Coys with their "moppers up" were responsible for the capturing of the 1st and 2nd Objectives including all remaining dug outs, trenches, communication trenches etc and including	

WAR DIARY
or
INTELLIGENCE SUMMARY

(Erase heading not required.)

7th R. INNISKILLING. Fus. Page 93.

Army Form C. 2118

Place	Date	Hour	Summary of Events and Information	Remarks and references to Appendices
In the Line	June 7		the 2nd objective. "C" and "D" coys with them hopped over reorganised for the capture of the RED and BLUE LINES, including all intervening ground, trenches, communication trenches etc from the 2nd Objective exclusive up to and including the 4th Objective. The following officers were wounded in the advance on the morning of the 7th :- 2/LIEUT. E. L. HENDERSON — "A" coy " " W. M. ELVERY — "D" " " " R. E. POYNTON — "D" " " " S. DICKSON — "B" " " " H. E. LINDE — "C" " " " W. S. BAKER — "A" " " " T. J. d'ALTON — "A" " " " C. W FAWKES — "C" " died of wounds 9th June. CAPTAIN. A.A. SEWARD — " " wounded at duty. " " " injured at duty. number of prisoners taken during the advance between 100 and 125. Two machine guns captured in good condition. Remainder of the day spent in consolidating the position.	

WAR DIARY or INTELLIGENCE SUMMARY

Army Form C. 2118

7th R. INNISKILLING FUS. Page 94

Place	Date	Hour	Summary of Events and Information	Remarks and references to Appendices

In the line

June 7th —

Total Casualties:-

	'A' Coy		'B' Coy		'C' Coy		'A' Coy		7 days		Total	
	Offs.	O.R.	Offs.	O.R.	Offs.	O.R.	Offs.	O.R.	Offs.	O.R.	Offs.	O.R.
A. Strength night 6/7th June	4	125.	4.	124.	5.	118.	4.	119.	5.	73.	22	559.
Do. 7/8th June	1	94.	3.	84.	4.	76.	2.	74.	5.	73.	15	401.
B. Killed	—	3.	—	3.	—	5.	—	3.	—	—	—	14
Died of Wounds	—	—	—	—	—	—	1.	5.	—	—	1	5
Wounded	3	26.	1.	28.	1.	37.	1.	32.	—	—	6	122.
" on duty	1	—	—	—	—	2.	—	—	—	1	1	3
Injured	—	2	—	1	—	1	—	4	—	1	—	16
Missing	—	—	—	10	—	—	—	—	—	—	—	16 ?
Totals	3.	31.	1.	41.	3.	44.	2.	44.	1.	1	9.	16 ?

at 7 a.m. an instruction received from Headquarters 49th INF. BDE. that the BATTALION would be withdrawn, and take over the portion of the CHINESE WALL between S.P. 13 and CHOW. STREET (Map Reference Sheet WYTSCHAETE 28 SW2 from N17 d.6.7 to N17 d. 8.3).

8th — Battalion commenced withdrawal at 7 a.m. at 4 P.M. the battalion were distributed in the fields between

Army Form C. 2118

WAR DIARY
or
INTELLIGENCE SUMMARY
(Erase heading not required.)

7 R. INNISKILLING Fus Page 95

Place	Date	Hour	Summary of Events and Information	Remarks and references to Appendices
In the Line	8th June		the BRYKERIE FARM (map Ref WYTSCHAETE 28 S.W.2 N17 & 7.5) and WILTSHIRE HOUSE (N17 & 7.8). Battalion Headquarters at THE FOSSE N16 d.2.4. June line between the BRYKERIE FARM and WILTSHIRE HOUSE.	
"	9th		at 3 P.M. the battalion moved to LOCRE to WICKLOW LINES. (map Ref sheet France 28 S.W. Ed. 5A M2 a. 5. 9. Battalion in reserve at 4.15 P.M. Battalion in WICKLOW LINES. nothing and cleaning up	
"	10th		Battalion furnished a working party of 500 other ranks for the purpose of road making. This party reported at point where the VIERSTRAAT	
"	11th		ROAD cuts our OLD front line (map Ref sheet WYTSCHAETE 28 S.W.2. 18 d. 7. 8.	
"	12th		from 6 A.M. the Battalion was held in readiness to move at 2 hours notice in case of a counter attack. The following was received from 16th DIVISIONAL COMMANDER:- "The 16th Division has been relieved to-day. For over eight months we have held our portion of the line in the SPANBROEK, VIERSTRAAT & DIEPENDAAL SECTORS and we can look back with pride and satisfaction to the record of those months. neither rain or snow, or the heat of Summer has interfered with the constant work, long distances, wet weather, cold nights, shortage of fuel, hostile shelling	

Army Form C. 2118

WAR DIARY or INTELLIGENCE SUMMARY

(Erase heading not required.)

7. R. INNISKILLING Fus. Page 96.

Place	Date	Hour	Summary of Events and Information	Remarks and references to Appendices
In the line	12 June		have all helped to cramp the spirits of our men. With gun and howitzer, hand mortar, rifle, machine gun and bomb and sometimes with Bayonet, we have gradually worn down the resisting enemy; and two days ago with a rush swarm to the finish, we have completed this chapter of our history by taking from him the WOOD and VILLAGE of WIJTSCHAETE, and the crest of the hill which means no end of future operations. The Divisional Commander in congratulating all ranks and all arms of the Division on their victory of June 7th, thanks all the officers, N.C.O's and men under his command for their loyalty and help, and for their bravery and skill in action. Whatever the Division may be called upon to do before us, it will be tackled with the same endurance, the same work and the same tenacity, and again and again the Division has never cheerfully and successfully carried out the fighting taking it on night in and night out. "always faithful."	
			June 9th 1917.	
			Extract from Batt. R.O. 2 11.6.17.	
			" Major General W.B. Hickie. C.B. commdg 16th Irish Div., has requested the commdg officer to make known to all ranks that as a mark of his appreciation of the gallant conduct shown by the Battalion on the morning of the 7th of June 1917 he had approved of the re-christening of UN NAMED WOOD as INNISKILLING WOOD and has given directions for a	
			(Sgd) W.B. Hickie, Major General	
			commdg. 16th Irish Division	

Army Form C. 2118

WAR DIARY
or
INTELLIGENCE SUMMARY
(Erase heading not required.)

7th R. INNISKILLING Fus 2 Page 97

Place	Date	Hour	Summary of Events and Information	Remarks and references to Appendices
In the Line	12 June		Leaving this morn: being erected therein. Officers on the strength of the Battalion are distributed and reported as follows with effect from 12th June 1917.	
			C.O. ---- LIEUT-COL. H.N. YOUNG, D.S.O.	
			2nd in Command ---- MAJOR. A.D. REID, D.S.O. (F)	
			Adjutant ---- CAPTAIN. A.E. TAGGART.	
			Asst " " ---- 2/LIEUT. A.H.H. ARMSTRONG.	
			" " " ---- " " H.P.H. MONTGOMERY.	
			Communication Officer ---- " " N.H. WOODS. M.C.	
			Intelligence & F/S Officer ---- CAPTAIN. S.O.F. ALLEY. M.C.	
			Medical Officer ---- LIEUT. W. REID.	
			Qr-mr ---- A/LIEUT. H.F. REID.	
			Transport Officer ----	
			'A' Company:-	
			CAPT. U.H. PARR. M.C. ---- Commdg Coy	
			2/LIEUT. J.S. FOLEY ---- 2nd in Command	
			A/" " T.H. SHAW ---- Platoon Comdr	
			" C.N.B. WALKER ---- " "	
			" J.F.C. O'BRIEN ---- " "	
			" W.T. SMYTH ---- " "	
			" O.W. HOLMES ---- " "	
			'B' Company:-	
			CAPT. D.H. MORTON ---- Commdg Coy	
			LIEUT. A.E.C. TRIMBLE ---- 2nd in Command	
			A/" " T.H. SHAW ---- Platoon Comdr	
			2/LIEUT. H.P. McKENNA ---- " "	
			" H.V. LOWRY ---- " "	

Army Form C. 2118.

WAR DIARY
or
INTELLIGENCE SUMMARY
(Erase heading not required.)

7th B. INNISKILLING Fus. Page 98

Place	Date	Hour	Summary of Events and Information	Remarks and references to Appendices
In the line	12 June		"C" Company:- "D" Company:-	
			A/Captain A.A. SEWARD — Comdg Coy Captain C.H. STAINFORTH — Comdg Coy	
			LIEUT. A.F.C. GRAVES — 2nd in command 2/LIEUT H.W. RUDDOCK — 2nd in Command	
			2/LIEUT J. CUNNINGHAM — Platoon Comdr. " " C.S. METCALFE — Platoon Commdr.	
			" " C.W. FAWKES — " " " " S. DOLAN — "	
			" " F.D. MORPHY — " " " " R.A. HEARD — "	
			2/LIEUT J.T. FLANAGAN — attached Bde as an additional Sigs Officer	
			" " H. LILLEY — Employed 2nd Army Scheme of musketry	
			2/LIEUT V.S. GWYNNE admitted to hospital on 19.5.17 was transferred to	
			ENGLAND on the 27.5.17 and is struck off the strength of the Battalion	
			accordingly, authy:- D.R.O 2734 of 5.6.17 and until 3rd Echelon of 6.6.17.	
			Batt. Operation Order re move to the MERRIS AREA about 2 miles S. of METEREN	
			about HAZEBROUCK Sheet 5A 1/100,000 issued to all concerned.	
MERRIS.	13th June		At 6 A.M. battalion released from duty as a unit ready to move at	
			2 hours notice.	
			Battalion started at 7 a.m. to march to MERRIS and Battalion HQ.pp	

Army Form C. 2118.

WAR DIARY
or
INTELLIGENCE SUMMARY.
(Erase heading not required.)

7th R. INNISKILLING Fus=   Page 99

Place	Date	Hour	Summary of Events and Information	Remarks and references to Appendices
MERRIS	13th June		Situated at F.2.6 3&7. Sheet France 36A. SE.6. Extract from Batt. R.O. 2/14.6.17:-	
"	14th "		"The C.O. on his own behalf, and on that of all ranks in the Battalion, congratulates the following gentlemen on being honoured on stated below by H.M. THE KING on the occasion of his Birthday:-	
			Major A.D. REID --- MENTION and Distinguished Service Order.	
			Capt. S. O.F. ALLEY } MILITARY CROSS. (Batt. medical officer)	
			CAPTAIN A.C. TAGGART } mentioned in Despatches. " A.A. SEWARD } REV. FATHER KELLY -- R.C. Chaplain (mentioned in Despatches). 15103 R.Q.M.S. WILSON R -- C" 21109 Sergt. STAFFORD. S -- "A" } mentioned in Despatches. 21178 Pte. O'DONNELL J -- "B"	
			The names of the following gentlemen have been brought specially to the notice of the C.O. in connection with the Battle of the 7th June on WYTSCHAETE RIDGE.	
			They have now been forwarded by him to the superior authority	

Army Form C. 2118.

WAR DIARY
or
INTELLIGENCE SUMMARY. 7 R. INNISKILLING Fusiliers Page 170

(Erase heading not required.)

Place	Date	Hour	Summary of Events and Information	Remarks and references to Appendices
MERRIS (Sheet 36A.226 F26 3½.7)	14 June		and he hopes that they will all get the honours which he considers they deserve.	
			CAPTAIN C.H. STAINFORTH ---- 'A' coy	
			2/LIEUT. H.W. RUDDOCK ---- 'A' "	
			" " F.D. MURPHY ---- 'C' "	
			" " H.P.H. MONTGOMERY ---- Hdqrs "	
			A/LIEUT. H.F. REID ---- Hdqrs "	
			26457 CORP. J. MAYNES ---- 'B' "	
			28674 " TAYLOR 'B' "	
			20175 Pte. J. CROWE ---- 'C' "	
			18116 Sergt. T.J. MORRIS ---- 'A' "	
			18409 Pte. C. WARD ---- 'B' "	
			13098 Sergt. T.A. CUNNINGHAM ---- Hdqrs "	
			26420 PTE (A/cpl) W. FAIRLESS ---- 'A' "	
			3286 " T. NORNEY ---- 'C' "	
			30199 Pte. E.H. SUTHERLAND 'C' coy, 20853 Pte. E. CHISHOLM 'D' coy, 20871	

WAR DIARY
INTELLIGENCE SUMMARY
7th R. INNISKILLING FUS. Page 101

Army Form C. 2118.

Place	Date	Hour	Summary of Events and Information	Remarks and references to Appendices
MERRIS	14 June		Pte M. SMITH. Hdqr. Coy. 25096 Pte J. DEEREY – D'Coy. 3174 Sergt R. DEELL – A'Coy	
"	"		28140 " M. SWEENEY – "B" Coy. 9178 Sergt F. HEANEY – Hdqr. 24898 Pte (A/Cpl) RIGLEY – Hdqr.	
"	"		15103 R.Q.M.S. WILSON – Hdqr. 21109 " S. STAFFORD– " 21230 Corpl. S.E. McGARRY. Hdqr.	
"	"		2/Lieut. J. E. O'BRIEN has been employed (temp) as asstant Qr-Mr with effect from 13th inst.	
			The following congratulatory messages were received by the Division from the Corps Commander :–	
			"The Army Commander wishes me to convey to all ranks his warmest congratulations and his appreciation of the splendid work they have done to-day (7th inst)"	
			"Well done 16th DIVISION. Heartiest congratulations on capture of WYTSCHAETE. I fully realise what a magnificent effort by each individual this has been."	
"	15 June		2/LIEUT. S. DOLAN returned from the Divisional Reinforcement Camp BERTHEN. and returned to his Coy. for duty.	
"	16 June		Battalion in MERRIS harours and resting. Operations Orders re moves	

Army Form C. 2118.

WAR DIARY
~~INTELLIGENCE SUMMARY.~~
(Erase heading not required.)

4th R. INNISKILLING FUS. Page 102.

Place	Date	Hour	Summary of Events and Information	Remarks and references to Appendices
MERRIS	16th JUNE		to CLARE CAMP (Map Ref. Sheet 28. M33 a 65.95) moved to all concerned.	
"	17th	"	Battalion started its march to CLARE CAMP. Head of the Battalion passing the starting point Sheet 27 N 82 X 20 e.B.B. Route being METEREN.	
CLARE CAMP (Sheet 28 M33a 65.95)			SCHAEXKEN. CROIX de POPERINGHE. Battalion reached CLARE CAMP at 9.45 a.m. Orders received from Bde. at 11.30 P.M. that the Brigade was marching back to the MERRIS area on the 18th inst. Orders as usual issued to all concerned.	
CLARE CAMP.	18th	"	The battalion started its march to the MERRIS Area at 5.25 a.m. passing the starting point, Sheet 28 M33 d 5.9, at 5.30 a.m. Route being CROIX de POPERINGHE — SCHAEXKEN — METEREN. Battalion arrived its billets in the MERRIS AREA at 8.45 a.m. Battalion Hdqrs. situated at F 2 c 3.2.7 Sheet 36 A 3d 6. FRANCE.	
MERRIS. Sheet 36 A France F 2 c 3.2.7			LIEUT. A.E.C. TRIMBLE proceeded to the 16th Inf. Base Depot. ETAPLES on Instruction. (Autly 49th Inf. Bde. SCC IX/22.9 d 15.5.17). Captain C.H. STAINFORTH proceeded to the 2nd Army Rest Camp, AMBLETEUSE	

Army Form C. 2118.

WAR DIARY
~~INTELLIGENCE SUMMARY~~

(Erase heading not required.) 7th R. INNISKILLING Fus. Page 103

Place	Date	Hour	Summary of Events and Information	Remarks and references to Appendices
MERRIS	18 June		Men Boulogne Fgt 14 days rest.	
" "	19 "		Battalion in MERRIS AREA.	
			The S.O.C. 49th INF Bde, Brig. Gen. P. LEVESON-BOWER inspected and addressed the Battalion at 12 noon. He congratulated the tunnelling officer & the many smart turn out of the men, and the smart and valour displayed by the Batt. during the attack on the 7th June 1917. Operation Orders re the move to EECKE map Ref France Sheet 27 Q 2 0 d.1.2 issued to all concerned.	
" "	20th June		The battalion started its march to EECKE area. The head of the Battalion passed the cross Roads at X 19 c.2.9. Sheet 27 Sivis B. Belgium and France. Route being X 19 c.2.9 - cross Roads WYTCHITZ - cross Roads W 16 c.0.0. 50 - ROUGE CROIX - CAESTRE - EECKE. Battalion arrived in billets at 9.30 a.m.	
EECKE AREA Sheet 27 S.E.	B Series 21st June		Battalion remained in the EECKE AREA on the 20th & 21st JUNE 1917. Orders re the move of the Battalion to the BRUXELLES AREA. Map Ref Sheet 27 1/40000 M 5 c 2.3. issued to all concerned.	

Army Form C. 2118.

WAR DIARY
or
INTELLIGENCE SUMMARY.
(Erase heading not required.)

7th R. INNISKILLING. June Page 107

Place	Date	Hour	Summary of Events and Information	Remarks and references to Appendices
EECKE AREA	22nd June		Battalion started its march to the BROXEELE Area to be billeted in BULYSSCHEURE Sheet 27 Ed.2. M.S.C. 85.45 at 4.55 a.m.	
			The head of the battalion passed the crossroads at P30a1.4. Sheet 27 Ed.2 The route being thro'Rueds P30d1.4 — ST. SYLVESTRE. CAPPEL — Road junction P14a5.5 — Road junction P13b5.0 — OXELAERE — BAVINGHOVE — ZUYTPEENE — Hunse to billets.	
			The Army commander (Gen. Sir Herbert PLUMER. G.C.M.G. K.C.B.) inspected the battalion on its march through ZUYTPEENE.	
			Battalion reached its billets at 10.30 a.m.	
BROXEELE AREA Sheet 27 Ed/2.	23rd June		Position of Battalion Hdqrs being M.S.C. 8.1.4 Sheet 27. Ed.2. Battalion rested during the remainder of the day. This march Reinforcement of 24 other ranks arrived from the 16th I.B.D. are taken on the strength of the Battalion accordingly 2/Lieut C.H. ELLIOTT. D'Coy (also S.R. 3rd Batt) admitted to 113 F.A. Ambulance Sick on 3rd June and evacuated to No 2 C.C.S. on the same night has been transferred to ENGLAND on the 9th June and is consequently	

WAR DIARY
or
INTELLIGENCE SUMMARY

(Erase heading not required.)

7 R. INNISKILLING. Fus Page 105

Army Form C. 2118.

Place	Date	Hour	Summary of Events and Information	Remarks and references to Appendices
BUYSSCHEURE FARM Sheet 27d2 XX5 c.8.4	23rd June		Other offrs the strength of this unit entry in Employmt No A 667 d 19.6.17 and D.R. 07852 d 22.6.17 2/LIEUT. J.S. FOLEY admitted to Hospital Sick on 13th June 1917 was evacuated to No 1 Aust CCS on the 15th June.	
" "	24th June		Battalion in billets in vicinity of BUYSSCHEURE. Training being carried out. Captain. J. D. F. ALLEY, M.C. Medical Officer to the Battalion granted leave to ENGLAND from 25.6.17 to 8.7.17. Captain J.B. CAVANAGH carried out the duties of Medical Officer to the Battalion. Captain J.H. PARR, M.C granted leave to ENGLAND from 20th June to 30th June 1917. Lieut & Qr. Mr W. REID granted leave to ENGLAND from 24th June to 4th July 1917.	
" "	25th June		Battalion in billets. Training being carried out. 2/LIEUT J.L. HENDERSON to be Temp LIEUT dated 3rd February 1917. (Authy London Gazette No 3011 d 5.6.17 and Bone orders No 31 d 21.6.17.)	

WAR DIARY or INTELLIGENCE SUMMARY

7th Royal INNISKILLING Fus. Page 106

Army Form C. 2118.

Place	Date	Hour	Summary of Events and Information	Remarks and references to Appendices
BUYSSCHEURE FARM	25th June		Ref page 94 of War Diary the following is the corrected list of casualties up to date — Extract from Batt. R.O. d. 25.6.17	
Sheet 27 Ed 2 M5 c 8.4.			Casualty list BATTLE of WYTSCHAETE (INNISKILLING WOOD) 7th June 1917	

	'A' Coy		'B' Coy		'C' Coy		'D' Coy	
	Officers	O.R.	Officers	O.R.	Officers	O.R.	Officers	O.R.
Strength night 6/7th June	4.	125.	4.	124.	5.	118.	4.	119.
Strength night 7/8th June	1.	94.	3.	84.	4.	76.	2.	74.
Killed	—	3	—	3	—	5	—	5
Died of wounds	—	1	—	2	—	1	—	2
Wounded	3.	27.	1.	35.	1.	36.	1.	38.
" at duty	—	1	—	1	—	3.	—	1
Injured " "	—	1	—	1	—	1	—	1
Missing	—	1	—	1.	—	—	—	—
Totals	3	30	1	41	3	45	2	46.

Grand Total of casualties 9 Officers and 163 Other ranks.

Roll of Honour. The following men were buried in Battalion Cemetery

Army Form C. 2118.

WAR DIARY
or
INTELLIGENCE SUMMARY.
(Erase heading not required.)

7 R. INNISKILLING Fus. Page 107

Place	Date	Hour	Summary of Events and Information	Remarks and references to Appendices
BUYSSCHEURES farm	June 25		on the LAITERIE Cemetery KEMMEL VIERSTRAAT ROAD Map Ref Sheet WYTSCHAETE 28 SW2 Ed.5.A. N16c 8.2. —	
			23981 Pte MAYNES. D. "D" Coy. 26448 Pte LANGAN. J. "B" Coy. 20243 Pte McDAID. J. — "C" Coy	
			30111 " BURTENSHAW. A. "A" " 24223. " KERNAN. R. "B" " 26869 " LANNIGAN. J. "C" "	
			18644 A/Cpl. SMITH. J. "B" " 30188 A/Cpl. HARRELL. W. "C" " 41235 " COOKSON. J. "C" "	
			30322 Pte TOZER. J. "C" " 30214 Pte WELLS. T. "D" " 28455 " COSTELLO. M. "D"	
			30129 " ALLEN. E. "A" " 41239 " HULME. P. "D"	
			29674 Pte DRUMM. J. "D" Coy. Buried on the Battlefield.	
			3663 " WILLIAMSON. J. "C" " D of W. 8.6.17 not yet registered burial place not yet viewed	
			30301 " CROWSON. S. "D" " D of W. 7.6.17 Grave No. 515(20) Buried by 19 M. DIV. Burial Party	
			24637 " BUCKLEY. J. "D" " D of W. 9.6.17 Buried in BAILLEUL Cemetery 10.6.17	
			25719 " BUNTING. A. "B" " " " " 13.6.17 " " " " " 14.6.17	
			30158 L/Cpl. EDWARDS. L. "B" " " " " 16.6.17 " " " " " 17.6.17	
			2/Lieut T.J. D'ALTON died of wounds at No 20. General Hospital. CAMIERS 9.6.17	

Army Form C. 2118.

WAR DIARY
or
INTELLIGENCE SUMMARY.
(Erase heading not required.) 7th R. INNISKILLING Fusiliers Page 108

Place	Date	Hour	Summary of Events and Information	Remarks and references to Appendices
BUYSSCHEURE FARM	25 June		and buried in ETAPLES Cemetery on 10th June 1917	
			2/Lieut H.E. LINDE died of wounds on 24-6-17. Buried in NO 53 E.E.S. BAILLEUL on 24-6-17. Buried in Battalion cemetery near the LAITERIE CEMETERY, KEMMEL. VIERSTRAAT ROAD on the 25th June (Map Ref Sheet WYTSCHAETE 28 SW2. N16 & Y.2) minus:- 28758 Pte DOHERTY. P -- "D" Coy 41221 " SOUTHERN.H --- "B".	
			"Good went the INNISKILLINGS who bravely fighting fell and cursed their gemies & cruelty death to tell. Proclaim their ever famous name — o Earth present his head. And in the land for which they fought sow them an everlasting guard."	
"	26th		Battalion in Musk Training being carried out.	
"	28d		2/Lieut T.E. JOHNSTON. having reported for duty on the 25th June on return from Sick Leave ENGLAND is taken on the strength of the Battalion accordingly and posted to "D" Coy. (Authy Barbarous Part 11 SH4 No 3/5/21 6/17. The undermentioned officers have been transferred to ENGLAND on the dates and for the reasons stated against their names	

Army Form C. 2118.

WAR DIARY
or
INTELLIGENCE SUMMARY.
(Erase heading not required.)

7th R. INNISKILLING Fus. Page 109

Place	Date	Hour	Summary of Events and Information	Remarks and references to Appendices
BUYSSCHEURE	26th June		and as struck off the strength of their unit accordingly.	
FARM	"28"	"	2/Lieut. S. L. HENDERSON — 9.6.17 Wounded 7.6.17	
			" W. M. ELVERY — 9.6.17 " 7.6.17	
			" S. DICKSON — 9.6.17 " 7.6.17	
			" R. E. POYNTON — 10.6.17 " 7.6.17	
			" W. S. BAKER — 9.6.17 " 7.6.17	
			(Auty List No 798 d 18.6.17) and Div. Routine Order 2872 d 24.6.17).	
" "	29th June		The Battalion inspected at its training area training by the Divisional commander MAJOR GENERAL W. B. HICKIE. C.B. from 8.45 a.m. to 10.45 a.m. Reinforcement of 5 other ranks arrived from 16th Inf. Base Depot is taken on the strength of the Battalion accordingly. Operation Orders re the move from BUYSSCHEURE on the 30th June issued to all concerned.	
ZUDAUSQUES	30th June		Battalion started on its march to ZUDAUSQUES (map Ref Sheet 27 A S E France W.2) passing the Battalion starting point Cross Roads 5.33 d 7.5 Sheet 27 B & 2 at 5.50 a.m. Order of march was Hdqrs, 'A' Coy, Band,	

WAR DIARY
or
INTELLIGENCE SUMMARY

(Erase heading not required.) 7th R. INNISKILLING Fus. Page 110

Army Form C. 2118.

Place	Date	Hour	Summary of Events and Information	Remarks and references to Appendices
ZUDAUSQUES	30 June		"B", "C" and "D" Coys. Transport Route march:-	
			ST. MOMELIN — STOMER — ST. MARTIN AU-LAERT — ZUDAUSQUES.	
			Battalion arrived in billets in the vicinity of ZUDAUSQUES at 9.30 a.m. Battalion Hdqrs situated at W.1.d.8.5. Shot 27 A.S.G. Remainder of the day spent resting after the march. Training in Units	

1-7-17.

H.Y. ????
Leit-Col
Commdg 7th Royal Inniskilling Fus.

R18

49/16

WAR DIARY.

FOR MONTH OF JULY, 1917.

VOLUME :- 18

UNIT :- 8th R. enniskilling Fusrs

WAR DIARY
or
INTELLIGENCE SUMMARY.

Army Form C. 2118.

7 R. INNISKILLING. two Page 111

Place	Date	Hour	Summary of Events and Information	Remarks and references to Appendices
ZUDAUSQUES	JULY 1st		Battalion billeted in and around ZUDAUSQUES (Map Ref Sheet France	
Sht 27 A.S.E. 1/20 and W2 and 3.			27 A.S.E. 1/20 and W 2 and 3.	
W 2 and 3.			Battalion Hdqrs situated at W.1.d.8,5.	
			Battalion training being carried out.	
			2/Lieut A.H.H ARMSTRONG ceased to be employed as an Assistant Adjt on the 30th June 1917, and returns to 'C' coy. for duty.	
			12 other ranks other off the strength of the battalion being evacuated outside the Divisional area.	
			Extract from Batt. R. O. 946 d 3.7.17:-	
			Casualties:- BATTLE OF WYTSCHAETE. (INNISKILLING WOOD 7.6.17).	
			" The undermentioned men previously reported missing on the 7th June 1917 are now officially reported as wounded on that date	
			41121 Pte SOUTHERN, H. — 'B' Coy.	
			28758 " DOHERTY, P — 'D' "	
			The number of missing on 7th June 1917 now reads NIL.	
			2/LIEUT. H.W. RUDDOCK, proceeding to G.H.Q. Lewis Gun School LE TOUQUET.	

WAR DIARY

Army Form C. 2118.

7 R. INNISKILLING Fus Page 112

Place	Date	Hour	Summary of Events and Information	Remarks and references to Appendices
2nd AUSQUES	1st July			
Shot 27 A. S.E W 2 and 3	to		On the 10th July 1917.	
			Reinforcement of 70 other ranks arrived from 16th I.B.D. on the 5th July and were taken on the strength of the Batt. accordingly. Major R.S. KERR. M.C reported for duty on the 4th July on return from Senior officers course, ALDERSHOT, is taken on the strength of the battalion accordingly.	
	6th July		Battalion moved from its billets in 2nd AUSQUES at 4 P.M on the 5th July to camp in TATINGHEM.	
TATINGHEM			Major R.S. Kerr M.C has been commanded command and Pay of "B" Coy from CAPT. D.H. MORTON with effect from 4 July.	
	7th "		Operation orders re move to the WINNEZEELE area issued to all concerned.	
			MAJOR R.S. KERR. M.C becomes the Senior Major of the Batt with effect from to-day	
			LIEUT S. DOLAN joined the 49th T.M.B for duty on the 7th JULY.	
			MAJOR A.D REID. D.S.O appointed to command the 1st Batt	

WAR DIARY
INTELLIGENCE SUMMARY

Page 113
7R INNISKILLING Fus.

Place	Date	Hour	Summary of Events and Information	Remarks and references to Appendices
	7 July		ROYAL IRISH RIFLES proceeded to join them on the 7th inst and 10 officers off the strength of the Batt. accordingly. 16th Div. 9/2/250 d. 6.7.17.	
			2/Lieut C W FAWKES to be assistant adjutant vice 2/Lieut A H H ARMSTRONG.	
On the March	8th		The battalion moved off at 6 AM and marched to WINNEZEELE remaining for the night in the RUBROUCH area. Route being ST. MARTIN-au-LAERT – ST OMER – ST MOMELIN – LEDERZEELE – Rd junction B19 d.7.4. Battalion billeted for the night in B 22, 23, 24 and 29 Sheet 27 1/40000	
	9th		The battalion completed its move to the WINNEZEELE area leaving the area junction at B18 b.05.90 Sheet 27 B.2 at 5.30 a.m. Route being ESQUELBECQ – WORMHOUDT Rd junction C 17 a.5.3 – KIEKEN PUT – LOOGEHOEK to camp in WINNEZEELE as at map	

Army Form C. 2118.

WAR DIARY
or
INTELLIGENCE SUMMARY.

(Erase heading not required.)

7th R. INNISKILLING. Fus. Page 114

Place	Date	Hour	Summary of Events and Information	Remarks and references to Appendices
WINNEZEELE Sheet 27 S.E N.E S11.a.95.4	9 July		reference Sheet 27 Ed II N.E S20.00 S11.a.95.4 arriving in Camp at 9.30 a.m	
	10th July		Reinforcement of 32 other ranks arrived and were taken on to strength of the Batt. secondary	
			Battalion during training	
	12th July		2/Lieut R.G. HEARD granted leave to ENGLAND from the 12th-22nd July.	
			Capt D.H. MORTON holds over the command of "B" Coy from Major R.S. KERR. M.C with effect from 13th July.	
			Lieut. A.F.C. GRAVES granted Leave to MARSEILLE from 12th to	
	19th July		2/Lieut H.V Lowry granted Leave to ENGLAND from the 19th to the	
	20th July		29th July 1917	
			Major J.G. Ross M.C. appointed 2nd in Command (temporary) to the Battalion	
			vice Major C.J. Reid D.S.O (T) with effect from 7.7.17 under See. I CDS 38th under see. I CDS 38th/5
			Lieut A.F.C. Graves authorised to wear badge of rank of Captain (auth DRO 2980/7)	

Army Form C. 2118.
Page 115
7th R. Inniskilling Fus.

WAR DIARY
or
INTELLIGENCE SUMMARY.
(Erase heading not required.)

Place	Date	Hour	Summary of Events and Information	Remarks and references to Appendices
WINNEZEELE	20th July		Three other ranks struck off the strength of the Batt. on being evacuated outside Divisional Area (Extract Bn.O.O. 20.7.17 No. 1062)	
Shut 27 NE				
J11.a.95.4	21st July		Two N.C.Os. proceed to XIX Corps Reinforcement Camp. Musketry Instructor an Platoon Commander + Bayonet fighting Instructor (Extract Br.O.O. 1068 of 21.7.17) Four other ranks struck off the strength of the Batt. there being classified "P.1." and transferred to 219 Empl. Coy. and one employed on traffic control (Br.O.O. 1070 of 21.7.17)	
	23rd July		Seven other Ranks struck off the strength, four evacuated outside Divisional Area, and three over 14 days in hospital. (Extract Br.O.O. 1075 of 23.7.17) 2nd Lieut. S. Dolan, attached 49th T.M. Battery, is struck off the strength of the Batt. accordingly with effect from 7.7.17 (auth. B.R.O. 230 of 25.6.17) One hundred and seven other Ranks reinforcements arrived from XIX Corps Reinforcement Camp, and taken on the strength of the Batt. 23.7.17 (B.R.O. 1081 of 23.7.17) 2nd Lieut. K. Lilley rejoined Battalion for duty on 23.7.17 from the 2nd Army School of Musketry, and is reported to "C" Coy. for duty.	
	24th July		One other rank evacuated outside Divisional Area and struck off the strength accordingly (B.R.O. 1083 of 24.7.17) Col. R.C. Eve Late 18th R. Dub. Fus. joined the Batt. and dined at Hdqrs. Mess.	

Army Form C. 2118.

Page 116
7R.B. Inniskilling Fus.rs

WAR DIARY
or
INTELLIGENCE SUMMARY.
(Erase heading not required.)

Place	Date	Hour	Summary of Events and Information	Remarks and references to Appendices
WINNEZEELE Sheet 27 N.E. J.11.c.9.5.+	25th July		2/Lieut. Joseph Fisher reported for duty to-day 25th inst., and is taken on the strength of the Batt.n accordingly and posted to "C" Coy. (auth. A.Gs. N20/27/57 of 20.7.17) 2/Lieut. H. Liley is transferred from "C" Coy. to "D" Coy. with effect from to-day. The following Officers and other ranks were awarded Irish Brigade Parchment Certificates for distinguished service and devotion to duty on the 7/9th June, 1917:-	
			Captain C.H. Stanforth M.C.	
			2/Lieut. Kev. Ruddock	
			13098 Sgt (A/c.S.M) Cunningham J. "D" Coy.	
			18116 Sgt. T.F. Morris "B" "	
			24487 Cpl. J. Maguire "B" "	
			28674 " J. Taylor "C" "	
			26240 Sgt. W. Fairless "A" "	
			2366 Pte. J. Norney "C" Coy.	
			26620 " P. Quigley "B" "	
			18409 " C. Ward "B" "	
			20175 " J. Crowe "A" "	
WATOU L.8.c.9.S. Sheet 27 5d 2.	26th July		The Battalion moved off at 6.25 a.m. and marched for WATOU no 2 area. Route being Cross roads J.12.6 8.7 (See starting point), WATOU, Cross roads N.	

WAR DIARY
or
INTELLIGENCE SUMMARY

Army Form C. 2118.

7th R. Innis. Fus: Page 117

Place	Date	Hour	Summary of Events and Information	Remarks and references to Appendices
WATOU	26th July		K.M.C. Crossroads L.1.C. to L.8.C.9.5 (Reference Sheet 27 2d.2. 1/40,000).	
L.8.C.9.5			The Battalion completed the march passing through the entrance gates at L.8.C.9.5. at Captain E.A. Hester Royal Inniskilling Fusiliers ordered to proceed from England on 21.7.17 on being posted to this Battn. (auth. A.G. 926947 of 17.7.17). Captain E.A. Hester reported for duty with this Battn. at the XIX Corps Reinforcement Camp on 22.7.17. Capt Hester is posted to "A" Coy and will assume duties of 2nd in Command. (B" R.O. 1104 of 26.7.17)	
	27th July		Thirty-two other ranks proceeded on attachment to 49th M.G. Coy. for carrying purposes (B" R.O. 1108 of 27.7.17) Reinforcements Seventy-Seven other ranks from XIX Corps Reinforcement Camp. reported for duty and taken on the strength accordingly.	
	28th July		Fifteen other ranks rejoined Battn. on the 27.7.17 from evacuation and are taken on the strength. Five other ranks proceed to Poperinghe to undergo a course of instruction in Gas.	

T.F.R. Innis. Fus.
Part 118

WAR DIARY
INTELLIGENCE SUMMARY

Place	Date	Hour	Summary of Events and Information	Remarks and references to Appendices
WATOU L.8.c.9.5.	28th July		22957 Pte McGrath J. "B" Coy died of pneumonia on 26.7.17 at No 11 C.C.S. Interpreter 2/Cl. Van-Beu-Heuvel attached to the Battn for accommodation and rations with effect from to-day and is attached to "B" Coy for messing. The undermentioned officers are authorised to wear the Badges of rank shown against their names under Section 1 of C.D.S. 384:- Lieut. N. K. Woods " J. J. Flanagan " J. Cunningham " C. B. Webster " N. T. McKenna Auth. 16 Div. No. A.1/161 and A.1/228 dru. D.R.O. 3055 of 27.7.17	
	29th July		2/Lieut. J. Finigan and 2/Lieut. R. A. L. Lindop have been posted to the Battalion on first Commission dating from the dates they report for duty and will be attached to "A" and "B" Coys. respectively. Auth. Adjt. G.H.Q. M.S. 510/16742 d/26.7.17).	

Army Form C. 2118.

WAR DIARY
or
INTELLIGENCE SUMMARY. 7th R. INNISKILLING. F. Page 1119.
(Erase heading not required.)

Place	Date	Hour	Summary of Events and Information	Remarks and references to Appendices
WATOU AREA L8 & 9.5 Sheet 27 Ed 2	1917 30th July		Lieut. Col. H.N. Young D.S.O. and 2 representatives of the 1st Batt of the Regiment visiting. Unit was encamped in the vicinity of FRUUEN. Sheet 27. F & R. Battalion encamped at WATOU. N°2. area L 8 & 9.5 Sheet 27 Ed 2. Training being carried out. The battalion started its march from the WATOU area at 10.45 P.M Battalion order of march was:- 'X emely' Sections Itelegn. Coy. A Coy. B " C " D " Battalion Reserve (Echelon 'B') Remainder of Hd.qr. Coy. Transport. The head of the battalion passed the road junction L9 c 1.9 Sheet 27 Ed 2 at 11.10 P.M. 200 yards distance was kept between companies, the Battalion Reserve and the Transport.	

Army Form C. 2118.

WAR DIARY
or
~~INTELLIGENCE SUMMARY~~

7th R. INNISKILLING Fus. Page 120

(Erase heading not required.)

Place	Date	Hour	Summary of Events and Information	Remarks and references to Appendices
On the march	30th July		Route was:—	
			ROAD JUNCTION L9 c 1.9 (Sheet 27 Ed 2)	
			— L 11 G 8.8 " " "	
			— GRANDE PLACE. POPERINGHE " " "	
			— MAIN. YPRES. ROAD. " " "	
			— "B" Camp 5 b d 4.4 (Sheet Belgium 28 N.W. Ed 5A 2000)	
"B" camp 5b d 4.4 Sheet 28 N.W. Ed 5A.	31st July		The battalion reached its new camp at 1.45 a.m. On arrival in camp the battalion came under two hours notice to move. Battalion in camp at 5 b d 4.4 Sheet 28 N.W. Orders received from Inf. Bde. Hdqrs. at 8.15 P.M. to move to camp at H 10 c Sheet 28. N.W. Ed 5A. Companies moved at 200 yards interval. The head of the battalion moved off from "B" camp at 8.45 P.M. and passed the Brigade Starting point at 9.5 P.M. Route was:— MAIN. YPRES. ROAD. — Bde Starting Point H 8 a 4.8 (Sheet 28 N.W. Ed 5A.)	

Army Form C. 2118.

WAR DIARY
or
INTELLIGENCE SUMMARY.
(Erase heading not required.)

7th R. INNISKILLING Fus. Page 121

Instructions regarding War Diaries and Intelligence Summaries are contained in F. S. Regs., Part II. and the Staff Manual respectively. Title pages will be prepared in manuscript.

Place	Date	Hour	Summary of Events and Information	Remarks and references to Appendices
Battle	31st July	1917	— VLAMERTINGHE	
March			— thence to camp at H.10.c.	
Camp H.10.c			Batteries arrived in its temporary camp at 11.45 P.M. and was reported present.	
Sheet 28 N.W. 3rd 5			The battalion on arrival in new camp was placed under one hours notice to move. A very wet and unfavorable night were spent in a barren and muddy field. During the night a German Infantry shell were reported to have hit the field occupied by the battalion. No damage or casualties occurred by the unexpected visit of the shell.	
			Strength on 1st July, 32 officers and 688 men. Strength on 31st July, 32 and 991 otherwise	
			Trench " 1st " " 24 " 639 Trench " 31st July, 30 " 823	

2-8-17.

M Murray
Lieut-Col.
Commdg 7th R. Innis Killing Fus.

Army Form C./2118.

WAR DIARY
or
INTELLIGENCE SUMMARY.
7th R.Inniskilling Fusrs.   page 122.
(Erase heading not required).

Vol 2 #19

Place	Date	Hour	Summary of Events and Information	Remarks and references to Appendices
Bivouac	1917 Aug 1		The battalion moved back to W. Camp, SHRAPNEL AREA C.6.d.4.4. sheet BELGIUM 28 N.W.	
			Owing to the very wet weather and lack of shelters at the Camp, about ¾ mile	
			S. E. of E of IMMERTI-COME.	
	" 2		In the above Camp	
	" 3		ditto	
	" 4		"	
	" 5		"	
	" 6		2nd Lieut T. E. Johnston, Bn Intelligence Officer went up to visit the O.P. & O.P. front	
			lines in the neighbourhood of the IRISH - ST JULIEN road; on returning about midday he was	
			slightly wounded and gassed, and admitted to hospital. The same evening the battalion	
			moved out and proceeded to the present front line passing through YPRES about 10 p.m. The	
			Battalion on the relief being completed (8 R.Innis Fus) held a line running roughly through	
			FROST HOUSE. i.e. about 400 yards N.W. of ST JULIEN - NEW FARM - and thence to the	
			STEENBEEK at a point about 150 yards S of the southern limits of the old german strong	
			Point, known as POMMERN CASTLE. BECK HO. about 150 yards in front of the left centre of the	
			Battalion was held by the Germans who had a m/G there. Bn H.Q's were at SQUARE FARM just over	

WAR DIARY
or
INTELLIGENCE SUMMARY.
7th R.Inniskilling Fusrs.

(Erase heading not required.)

Army Form C. 2118.

Place	Date	Hour	Summary of Events and Information	Remarks and references to Appendices
			500 yards from the Cross roads at FREZENBERG and about 350 - 400 yards behind the line held by us. This farm had been strongly concreted inside and had about 5 feet of reinforced concrete on top. It had apparently originally been made as an Aid Post by the Germans. on its southern front was a veranda about 8 feet broad running its entire length with about 1 foot of concrete overhead cover, the ends only of this veranda were open. The accommodation was not suitable for more than 100 men at a pinch. 1 section of the 49th M.G. Coy under 2nd Lieut Joyce were stationed here.	
			There was a supply of good well water about 10 yards away. From this farm there was a very fine view of the country all round excepting our own front line which was in the dip. IBERNIA Fm, DELVA FARM, ZEVENCOTE, COFFEE FARM, HILL 37 etc being all visible, as also POMMERN CASTLE on the north & FREZENBERG on the south ST JOSEPH'S INSTITUTE, the Railway embankment between the latter place and ZONNEBEKE, ZONNEBEKE itself. The map shows clearly the configuration of the ground, which was remarkably open and free from natural obstructions, hedges trees etc.	
			All 4 companies of the Bn were in the line, A Coy being on the right. There was a gap of about 100 yards between our B Coy and the right Company of the Ulster Division on our left.	

Army Form C. 2118.

WAR DIARY
or
INTELLIGENCE SUMMARY.
7th R.Inniskilling Fusrs. Page 124.

(Erase heading not required.)

Instructions regarding War Diaries and Intelligence Summaries are contained in F. S. Regs., Part II. and the Staff Manual respectively. Title pages will be prepared in manuscript.

Place	Date	Hour	Summary of Events and Information	Remarks and references to Appendices
B.Q. RM YPRES	7		In this gap in the trench, the Germans were reported to place a m/G at any rate by night. 2nd Lieut R.A.Heard "D" Coy wounded and at duty on the 8th, he reported sick and was sent to Hospital.	
		6-55 p.m.	Intense Artillery fire by Germans all along the British front, enemy reported to have attempted a raid on our immediate right; our casualties 8 O.R's wounded, these slight casualties being due to the enemy not having got our front line range accurately. One	
"	8.8.17.		M/G at H.Q.'s was destroyed and two temporarily put out of action. Enemies shells chiefly 4.2's with a good sprinkling shot of 5.9's. The situation became normal again about	
		9-45 p.m.	2nd Lieut & A/Lieut T.H.Shaw and Sgt Carroll both of "B" Coy, during this bombardment in moving forward to their front line of shell holes & old trenches (German) presumably lost their bearings and wandered into the German lines, where presumably they were captured. 2nd Lieut G.J.Metcalfe was also injured in his right hand by a piece of old German barbed wire.	
	9th		Nothing special happened.	
	10th		2nd Lieut R.Lilley was slightly wounded and also 2nd Lieut M.T.Smith, both remained at duty. During this period in the line the battalion had a far more uncomfortable time than they	

A6945 Wt. W14142/M1160 350,000 12/16 D. D. & L. Forms/C.2118/14.

WAR DIARY
or
INTELLIGENCE SUMMARY.

(Erase heading not required.)

7th R.Inniskilling Fusrs.

Army Form C. 2118.
Page 125.

Place	Date	Hour	Summary of Events and Information	Remarks and references to Appendices
			had ever experienced before, they were continuously subjected to intermittent artillery fire of a heavy nature from 4.2's & 5.9's. They were unable to move an inch by day owing to snipers and m/g's, roughly from 4-15 a.m. to 9 p.m. there was no intercourse whatsoever between Companies and Bn H.Q's or even between platoons of the same Company. Men had to sit tight and not move or show themselves or they were promptly sniped at and the trenches or shell holes they were in were all waterlogged. Bn H.Q's itself was used, one might almost say, as a target for the calibration of guns of all weights by the Germans. The FREZENBERG Ridge, about 350 yards S of it and the FREZENBERG - SQUARE FM - BRIDGE HO.road had at uncertain but frequent intervals for short or long periods heavy barrages put down on them.	
	10/11 Aug		On this night the Battalion moved out to TORONTO CAMP, about ¾ miles S.W. of BRANDHOEK entraining at the ASYLUM, YPRES. During the above period the Casualties were:	
			K. W. W.at duty. M.	
			Officers. - 2 3 1 - 6	
			O.R's) 10 50 5 6 - 71	
			10. 52. 8. 7. - 77.	

Army Form C. 2118.

WAR DIARY
or
INTELLIGENCE SUMMARY.

7th R.Inniskilling Fusrs.   Page 125.

(Erase heading not required.)

Place	Date	Hour	Summary of Events and Information	Remarks and references to Appendices
			For their services during the above period in the front line the following O.R's were recommended as stated below for decorations.R.409. d/14.8.17.	
			23011 Corporal William BURKE. D.C.M.	
			20578 Private John FENTON M.M.	
			22536 " Mattheis McGRATH. M.M.	No1 recommended by Brig 9 m. hour dij PS 1st 7.8 etc
			43275 " (L/Cpl) Charles BENNET. M.M.	ditto.
			4069 " John TOLAND. M.M.	
BRAND-HOEK Area	12		2nd Lieut H.P.H.MONTGOMERY,Communication Officer, admitted through 113 rd Ambulance to a C.C.S. sick.	
TORONTO CAMP.	13		Captn & Adjt A.C.TAGGART, admitted through 113 rd amb to a C.C.S. sick.	
			2nd Lieut C.W.D.WALKER. A Coy and 2nd Lieut C.W.RUDDOCK. D Coy authorised to wear the badges of rank of Captains,whilst acting as such. Auth G.R.O. 2494. d/5.8.17 and Bde R.O. 2272. d/24.8.17.	
			Captain E.H.Hester, appointed A/Adjutant,temporary.	

Army Form C. 2118.

WAR DIARY
or
INTELLIGENCE SUMMARY.

(Erase heading not required.)

7th R.Inniskilling Fusrs.   Page 127.

Place	Date	Hour	Summary of Events and Information	Remarks and references to Appendices
BRAND-HOEK AREA. TORONTO CAMP.	1917 Aug 14.		Battalion moved forward into its preparatory positions for the attack on the 16th inst. The Officers being, C.O. Lt Col A.D.YOUNG, D.S.O; A/2nd in Comm,Captn V.H.PARR, M.C; A/Adjt Captn E.L.HESTER; for general duties,2nd Lieut C.W.FAWKES; Medical Officer,Captain G.O.F.ALLEY, M.C; A Coy,2nd Lieut & A/Captn C.N.B.WALKER, 2nd Lieuts W.T.SMYTH and C.W.HOLMES - B Coy,Captn D.H.MORTON, 2nd Lieuts and A/Lieuts M.H.WOODS,M.C. and H.P.McKENNA, 2nd Lieut H.V.LOWRY - C Coy,Lieuts and A/Captn A.F.C.GRAVES, 2nd Lieuts A.H.H.ARMSTRONG, F.D.MORPHY, J.FISHER - D Coy,2nd Lieut & A/Captn H.W.RUDDOCK, 2nd Lieut & A/Lieut J. CUNNINGHAM, 2nd Lieuts R.A.HEARD and H.TILLEY. The W.O's being Sgt & A/R.S.M. T.CUNNINGHAM. Companies had no W.O's or A/W.O's with them, C.S.M.DUNNE of D Coy having been wounded on the 7.8.17. Bn H.Q's were at SQUARE FARM, A & C Coy reading from S to N held the northern portion of the Bn frontage as occupied by the Bn between the 6th and 16th inst; the southern portion being held by the 8th R.Innis Fus,with its H.Q's also in SQUARE FARM with two Companies. B & D Coys were in support in the O.G. 2nd line	
SQUARE FARM. S.of N of YPRES.		9.15	Battalion in same position till 10-30 p.m. when it commenced moving into its assembly positions prior to the attack on the morning of the 16th inst (it must be distinctly understood that no intercourse had been possible between Bn H.Q's and its two front Companies,	

WAR DIARY
or
INTELLIGENCE SUMMARY.

(*Erase heading not required.*)

7th R.Inniskilling Fusrs.

Army Form C. 2118.

Page 128.

Place	Date	Hour	Summary of Events and Information	Remarks and references to Appendices
	15		C and A from dawn in the morning until about 8-30 p.m. that night.	
			C Coy stood fast. A Coy was relieved by a Company of the 7/8th R.I.F. and moved into position behind "C" Coy.	
			D & B Coys moved up from the rear through SQ Fm into their positions on the northern side of the DAWDLER (STEENBEEK) in continuation of the line occupied by C and A Coys respectively, linking up with the Coys of the 9th R.I.F. (Ulster Division) under Major & Temp Lt Col S.J. SOMERVILLE. The line so taken up by them being strictly speaking in the Ulster Div area, but special leave had been given to the Battn to use, so as to simplify its advance, there being streams which might have impeded its advance on its objectives otherwise.	
			It was not till after D & B Coys had passed on H.Q's. i.e. about 11 p.m. that ZERO hour, viz. 4.45 a.m. for the following day was received. Platoons of the 7/8th R.I.F. also moved into allotted positions behind the first wave and Bn H.Q's of the 8 R.Innis Fus moved out/into LOW FARM. Whilst that of the 7/8th R.I.F. moved in. The number of M/G's was also brought up to 12 under Lieut COLLINSON and a new art. liason officer Lt............ reposted himself.	
	16	2-30 a.m.	Everything was ready as far as the Battalion was concerned, all last orders etc including ZERO time having had to be given verbally to the O.C's C & A Coys owing to their being in	

Army Form C. 2118.

WAR DIARY
or
INTELLIGENCE SUMMARY.

7th R.Inniskilling Fusrs.   Page 129.

(Erase heading not required.)

Instructions regarding War Diaries and Intelligence Summaries are contained in F. S. Regs., Part II. and the Staff Manual respectively. Title pages will be prepared in manuscript.

Place	Date	Hour	Summary of Events and Information	Remarks and references to Appendices
		4-45 a.m.	position when it was impossible to show a light.	
			The Battle started, the enemies barrage replying within a minute. Companies advanced splendidly	
			they had already rushed the lone M/G noted above and were well in front of their own lines	
			before the enemies barrage fell (every man knew his objective and had had the objectives etc	
			of the Bn thoroughly ground into him, whilst every N.C.O. L/Cpls included, together with all	
			Signallers and Runners had visited the Corps Model and had the position and lay of the ground	
			over which they were to attack thoroughly explained to them)	
		5.05 a.m.	The Battn could be seen in its allotted position on the GREEN line. The troops on its left	
			appeared also to be going strong. The situation on the right did not appear quite so	
			satisfactory but nevertheless BECK HOUSE having been reported as captured, the brigade was	R.2.
		5-30 a.m.	informed that the attack was going strong.	R.3.
		5.50 a.m.	at 5.50 a.m. the troops on our left still appeared to be advancing but not so strongly.	
			They were then apparently by GALLIPOLI FARM. The Battalion itself were through DELVA FARM.	
			but the 8th R.Innis Fus were being held up by m/G fire, the latter was reported to brigade	
			at 5-50 a.m.	
		6.05 a.m.	It was reported to the brigade that the wounded were coming in in large numbers, all belonging	R.4.

Army Form C. 2118.

WAR DIARY
or
INTELLIGENCE SUMMARY.

(Erase heading not required.) 7th R.Inniskilling Fusrs.   Page 130.

Place	Date	Hour	Summary of Events and Information	Remarks and references to Appendices
			to the Battalion "all report however that the attack is going well".	
		6.12 a.m.	Following wire sent Bde. "according to report DELLVa FARM captured, time 5-36 a.m.	R.4
		7.01 a.m.	Report sent Bde. "Report from DELLVa FM states 36th Div have a rumour that the Division on their left has retired, please investigate and inform me aaa mopping up reported not satisfactory and there is a lot of sniping going on behind my front lines aaa is not satisfied with general state of affairs as reported aaa no communication established except by runner".	R.7.
		7.15 a.m.	The above report was confirmed from the O.C. my A/an H.Q's, Captn Parr, M.O. who in a message timed 6-25 a.m. stated "The mopping up has been bad and there are a number of the enemy in our rear. My B Coy was then digging itself in 50 yards N of DELLVa.	
		7.55 a.m.	8 R.Innis Fus reported in reply to my R.6. "We have not had any news at all except that we were held up by M/G's at BORRY FARM, this was received at 8-30 a.m.	
		8.12 a.m.	Meanwhile Maj Scott and 2 R.I.R. less 1 Coy had arrived in our old front line. Having noticed my self and judging by reports of the wounded I instructed him to send a Company from our front line near BEck No. to clear BORRY FARM. This Company failed as also had a Company of the 7/8 R.I.F.	
		9.21 a.m.	Following message sent to Bde. "Battalion has been forced to retire, want of support aaa casualties CO, D/CO, Pat, believed killed aa KY".	R.22.

D. & L. Forms/C/2118/14.

Army Form C. 2118.

WAR DIARY
or
INTELLIGENCE SUMMARY.
(Erase heading not required.)

7th R.Inniskilling Fusrs.   Page 131.

Instructions regarding War Diaries and Intelligence Summaries are contained in F. S. Regs., Part II and the Staff Manual respectively. Title pages will be prepared in manuscript.

Place	Date	Hour	Summary of Events and Information	Remarks and references to Appendices
		9.40 a.m.	Following message sent to Bde. "Situation very bad. Men retiring all over the place, have you received my wires, are you sending supports up. Please acknowledge all wires as I have received no answer yet. Urgent"	R.23
		10.50 a.m.	8 R.Innis Fus.report timed at 10-50 a.m. "Wounded Officers of this Battn says we have had very bad time and we are badly cut up as I do not think it possible for us for any length of time as am still at LOW FARM" (note: message not clear).	3/90.
		10.30 a.m.	Reported to Bde "that we now hold roughly the original line but including BECK HOUSE etc etc.	
		11.10 a.m.	As no message whatsoever had been received from the Bde since the commencement of the action reported direct to Div as follows: "I cannot get through to my brigade or get any word from them by runner or otherwise as the situation is serious, apparently we took our objectives, Hill 37 and BELVA FARM, but the 9 R.I.F. of 36th Div. gave way before a Counter-attack and left the battalion with both flanks in the air. The 8 R.Innis Fus having been held up apparently by BURRY FARM. The remains of the whole brigade now hold our original front line including BECK HOUSE, but are very disorganised. I fear we could not hold this line without reinforcements. Casualties very heavy. Have sent Maj Scott to try further and reorganise line xxxxx."	R.26.

WAR DIARY
or
INTELLIGENCE SUMMARY.

7th R.Inniskilling Fusrs.   Page 132.

Army Form C. 2118.

Place	Date	Hour	Summary of Events and Information	Remarks and references to Appendices
	16	1.30 p.m.	About 1.30 p.m. The first message since the commencement of the battle was received by me. their D.M.O. 5tb d/16.8.17. It made no reference to the numerous messages sent to the brigade but was merely a direct order at all costs to take BORRY FARM:-	
			"The 2nd Dublins hold from D.26 central to just west of BREMEN REDOUBT which is held by Germans. The 49th Infy Bde hold BECK HOUSE. The 8 R.Innis Fus will make their strength up to 300 strong calling on C.O's battalions holding our line (7 R.Innis Fus, 7/8 R.Ir Fus & 2nd R. Irish Regt) for men. With these men 8 R.Innis Fus will attack BORRY FARM, garrison it and push forward as far as the river, joining up on the right with 2 Dublins West of BREMEN REDOUBT. The left to be east of BORRY FARM. Touch with garrison of BECK HOUSE must be maintained. This attack must be carried out at all costs to support 2 Dublins at the order of the Div Comdr. C.O. 8 R.Innis Fus will notify Bde H.Q's the hour he is ready to attack. The H.R. are firing on BORRY FARM and will be switched off as soon as hour for attack is notified. The message giving the hour must be sent by two different runners. If the power buzzer is working, the message will be sent by this means also artillery support is being arranged for to start at the hour notified".	
			This was not a practical order and simply proved that the brigade H.Q's behind had not the	

WAR DIARY
or
INTELLIGENCE SUMMARY.

(Erase heading not required.) 7th R.Inniskilling Fusrs. Page 133.

Army Form C. 2118.

Place	Date	Hour	Summary of Events and Information	Remarks and references to Appendices
			slightest conception of the situation. Here it might be noted that my own Trspt Officer Lieut H.F.Reid came up with Pack Transport with Ammn and returned safely, and further that I sent two officers back to report on the situation, besides numerous runners.	
			The following reply was sent (the 8 R.Innis Fus being at the same time instructed to make their preparations) :-	R.33.
			"Ref your B.M.G.515. There are no 7 R.Innis Fus left in any formation. The 2 R.I.R. are fairly well in hand. The 8 R.Innis Fus are not in too good form and I am not sure that they are sure of their own location. The 7/8 R.I.F. are fairly in hand also. BECK HOUSE has been evacuated. I propose that I Coy 7/8 R.I.F. retake BECK HO. and that the 8 R.Innis Fus are stiffened as reqd by men from the 2 R.I.R. leaving only the remnants of the 7/8 R.I.F. in support. I fear the operation proposed by you has little chance of success. The men are done in L/G's lost etc".	R.34.

WAR DIARY
or
INTELLIGENCE SUMMARY.

7th A.Iniskilling Fusrs.   Page 134

Army Form C. 2118.

Place	Date	Hour	Summary of Events and Information	Remarks and references to Appendices
	6.6.17	3.27 p.m.	The order re the counter-attack was cancelled by D.M.C. 515 timed 1.20 p.m. but not received until 3.27 p.m.	
			Meanwhile the situation at BECK HOUSE was indefinite, apparently from later information neither side held it, but both had a few troops facing it about 150 yards apart with this place in the centre.	
		2.35	A report from the 8 R.Innis Fus timed 2.12 p.m. stated they were holding a broken line 100 yards N of BORRIE FARM, and that this farm was causing them casualties from snipers and m/g's.	R.36
			This line eventually turned out to be held by both 7th and 8th R.Innis Fus. 2nd Lieut A.H.H. Armstrong of the 7th coming in from it via BECK HQ. which he actually entered and when he saw numerous wounded both of our troops and the Germans, the time would be about 3-15 p.m.	
		3.15	The Bde was then informed that it was to be relieved, excepting the 2 R.Ir Regt who would divide the front line with the relieving battalion again proving that the Bde did not realise the state of affairs in front. The Battalion itself was to move to the ECOLE near YPRES.	
			This order was cancelled on a new strong memo being sent both by myself and Maj Scott Commdg 2 R.Ir Reg. In my R.31 timed at 1 p.m. it had been clearly pointed out that it was taken for granted that the brigade must be relieved and that "Relieving troops must take over brigade	

WAR DIARY
or
INTELLIGENCE SUMMARY. 7th R.Inniskilling Fusrs.

Army Form C. 2118.

Page 137.5

Place	Date	Hour	Summary of Events and Information	Remarks and references to Appendices
			frontage, impossible to take over from ens". Finally the brigade was relieved as suggested and the Bn moved back into the O.B. front line on the right of the road from YPRES to ZONNEBEKE. The strength of the battalion approximately at 4-45 a.m. on the morning of the 16.8.17. was:-	
			Officers. Men.	
			Bn H.Q's. 4 47.	
			A Coy. 4 113	
			B " 4 112	
			C " 4 104	
			D " 4 96.	
			20. 472.	

Army Form C. 2118.

WAR DIARY
or
INTELLIGENCE SUMMARY.

(Erase heading not required.)

7th R.Inniskilling Fusrs.   Page 138.

Place	Date	Hour	Summary of Events and Information	Remarks and references to Appendices
			The casualties during the fighting on the 16th were:-	
			Killed. Wounded. Missing. W & msg. msg believed K. D of Wounds. Off. O.R's. Off. O.R's. Off. O.R's. Off. O.R's. Off. O.R's. Off. O.R's.	
			H.Q's: - 3 1 12 - 3 - - - - - -	2. 18
			A Coy - 10 3 46 2 32 1 2 - - - -	9. 91
			B " - - - 43 1 28 1 6 1 6 - -	3. 83
			C " 1 11 3 46 - 33 - 3 - - - -	4. 93
			D " - 10 1 46 - 23 - 3 - - - -	1. 83
				16. 368
			2nd Lieut & A/Lieut J.T.Flanagan. attached pde signals. missing.	

WAR DIARY
or
INTELLIGENCE SUMMARY. 7th R.Inniskilling Fusrs.

Army Form C. 2118.

(*Erase heading not required.*)

Place	Date	Hour	Summary of Events and Information	Remarks and references to Appendices
			The Casualties amongst Officers were:	
			H.Qrs:	
			Captn & 2/2nd in Comm. G.V.PARR, M.C. Wounded. Flesh wound in leg.	
			Captn & A/Adjutant. B.A.FOSTER. Missing. Last seen unwounded at DELVA FARM.	
			"A" COY:	
			2nd Lieut & A/Captn C.E.C.WALKER. Wounded (twice) and missing.	
			2nd Lieut. W.T.SMYTH. Wounded.	
			" " C.W.HOLMES. Missing.	
			" " F.FINNIGAN. Wounded.	
			"D" COY:	
			Captn D.R.MORTON. Wounded and missing.	
			2nd Lieut & A/Lieut W.M.WOODS, M.C. " " believed killed,	
			seen to fall near DELVA Fm trying to rally his men whilst they were being pushed back.	

WAR DIARY
or
INTELLIGENCE SUMMARY.

7th R. Inniskilling Fusrs.   Page 138.

Army Form C. 2118.

Place	Date	Hour	Summary of Events and Information	Remarks and references to Appendices
			"C" COY: Lieut & a/Captn A.F.CARRIVES. Missing believed killed.	
			2nd " F.D.MORPHY. Wounded. Remained at duty till the 26th inst, when admitted to C.C.S. to undergo operation for the removal of fragments of a shell.	
			2nd Lieut. J.FISHER. Wounded.	
			"D" COY: 2nd Lieut & a/Captn H.W.RUDDOCK. Wounded and missing.	
			" " & a/Lieut J.CUNNINGHAM. Wounded.	
			" " R.A.E.LINDOP. " at duty.	
			Attached Brigade as } 2nd Lieut & a/Lieut J.T.Flanagan. Missing. Last seen firing a forward Bde Sig offcr.} M/G at Inshnia.	
			Serv'd with 49T-M.B. 2nd Lieut J Dolan Missing	

WAR DIARY
or
INTELLIGENCE SUMMARY.

7th R.Inniskilling Fusrs. Page 139.

Army Form C. 2118.

Place	Date	Hour	Summary of Events and Information	Remarks and references to Appendices
			In connection with the fighting on this date, 16th Augt 1917, the following recommendations were made:	
			1. Captn & a/2nd in Comm. V.H.PARR, M.C. For a Distinguished Service Order.	
			2. 2nd Lieut. F.D.MORPHY. For a Military Cross.	
			3. " " & A/Captn. G.N.B.WALKER. " "	
			4. 23618 Cpl. F.SMITH. For a Distinguished Conduct Medal.	
			5. 24228 Pte J.LOBLEY. " "	
			6. 5666 Sgt R.YOUNG. " "	
			7. 9644 Sgt W.ARMSTRONG. For a Military Medal.	
			8. 30120 Pte W.THOMPSON. " "	
			9. 26773 " D.ORMSBY. " "	
			10. 2754 Sgt R.ARMSTRONG. " "	
			11. 9818 Pte (Lce Cpl) T.McCORMICK. " "	

WAR DIARY
or
INTELLIGENCE SUMMARY.

(Erase heading not required.) 7th A.Inniskilling Fusrs. Page 140.

Army Form C. 2118.

Place	Date	Hour	Summary of Events and Information	Remarks and references to Appendices
	12.		Pte G.BURRELL.	For a military medal.
	13.		13096 Sgt & A/R.S.M. T.CUNNINGHAM.	" "
	14.		10691 Pte (Lce Cpl) A.ADAMS.	" "
	15.		21109 Sgt J.STAFFORD.	" "
	16.		24027 Pte (Lce Cpl) M.FIVEY.	" " Not forwarded by Bde gentleman to be + field inf sale
	17.		24456 Sgt P.MCTAGGART.	" "
	18.		2821 Cpl J.JACKSON.	" "
	19.		45211 Pte J.COULAN.	" "
	20.		41822 " H.J.COLES.	" "
	21.		26285 Cpl J.SCOTT.	" "
	22.		26309 Pte W.McILWRATH.	" "
	23.		26994 Pte J.McCALLION.	" "

Army Form C. 2118.

WAR DIARY
or
INTELLIGENCE SUMMARY. 7th R. Inniskilling Fusrs. Page 141.
(Erase heading not required.)

Place	Date	Hour	Summary of Events and Information	Remarks and references to Appendices
			Captn & a/Maj. J.D.SCOTT.	
			2nd R.Ir Regt. For a Distinguished Service Order. 16.8.17.	
			2nd Lieut JOYCE.	
			49th M/G Coy. For a Military Cross. For his work on the night of the 7/8th Aug.	
			Lieut COLLINSON.	
			49th M/G Coy. For a Military Cross. For 16.8.17.	
			Lieut Artillery Liason Officer, Attd on H.Q's SQUARE FM. "Gen Staff.XIXth Corps. G.904/30.	
			16th.Division. 21st Aug 1917.	
			In bidding Goodbye to the Division, the Corps Commander wishes to express his deep appreciation of the fine work done by all ranks during the time the Division has been with the XIXth Corps.	
			It was unfortunately necessary for the Division to take over the line and to hold it for over	

Army Form C. 2118.

WAR DIARY
or
INTELLIGENCE SUMMARY.

(Erase heading not required.)   7th R.Inniskilling Fusrs.   Page 142.

Instructions regarding War Diaries and Intelligence Summaries are contained in F. S. Regs., Part II. and the Staff Manual respectively. Title pages will be prepared in manuscript.

Place	Date	Hour	Summary of Events and Information	Remarks and references to Appendices
			"A fortnight before the attack in the worst of weather under constant shelling and almost nightly gas attacks, but in spite of all hardships and very large casualty lists, the Division carried out its preparation for the offensive without a pause and although the attack when it took place was not successful - very possibly due to the previous hardships undergone by the troops - it was an attack over very difficult country against the best troops in the German army and against a hitherto untried system of defence, and the Division may well be proud of the many gallant and heroic acts performed by so many of its officers and men. Their efforts were not thrown away, as the experience gained should prove of great value in coming attacks.	
			(Sd) F.LYON, Brig Gen.	
			Gen Staff, XIXth Corps.	
			21st Augt 1917".	
			Bde R.O. 2290. d/26.8.17. RECENT OPERATIONS:	
			The following copies of Letters from the Commander-in-Chief and the H.Q. of Fifth Army respectively are inserted for the information of all ranks:-	

Army Form C. 2118.

WAR DIARY
or
INTELLIGENCE SUMMARY.

(Erase heading not required.)

7th R.Inniskilling Fusrs.   Page 143.

Place	Date	Hour	Summary of Events and Information	Remarks and references to Appendices
			"No O.A. 830/12.	
			General Headquarters,British Armies in France.	
			17th Augt 1917.	
			General Sir H.de.la P.Gough, K.C.V.O., K.C.B.	
			Commanding Fifth Army.	
			I wish to congratulate you personally,as well as the Commanders,staffs and troops under your	
			command,most warmly on the successes gained by the Fifth Army yesterday,under conditions of	
			great difficulty and in the face of the most determined opposition.	
			The bad weather which delayed the continuance of our offensive enabled the enemy to bring up	
			and concentrate considerable forces in reserve and to make careful preparations to meet our	
			attack yesterday. In spite of this the determination and gallantry of the troops under your	
			command succeeded in striking another of the successful blows, the cumulative effects of which	
			are shattering the enemy's power of resistance and will ultimately lead to his complete	
			defeat.	
			(Sd) D.Haig. Field Marshall.g	
			"Fifth Army No. G.A. 790/9.	
			dated 19.8.17.	
			1. The attached copy of a letter received by the Army Commander from the Commander-in-Chief	

Army Form C. 2118.

WAR DIARY
or
INTELLIGENCE SUMMARY.

(Erase heading not required.)   7th R.Inniskilling Fusrs.   Page 144.

Instructions regarding War Diaries and Intelligence Summaries are contained in F. S. Regs., Part II. and the Staff Manual respectively. Title pages will be prepared in manuscript.

Place	Date	Hour	Summary of Events and Information	Remarks and references to Appendices
			is forwarded for your information (see above).	
			2. The Army Commander wishes it to be published for the information of all ranks, and at the same time to express his congratulations to Commanders, Staffs, and the troops under their Command, on the successes gained on the 16th instant.	
			3. He particularly wishes to express his deep admiration of the gallant determination and great spirit shown by the troops under the recent trying conditions of bad weather, and in face of stubborn resistance by the enemy. It is this splendid spirit of determination to win which is fast contributing to the defeat of our enemy.	
			(Sd) N.MALCOLM.	
			Major General, G.S.	
			Captain Henry Victor FARR, M.C. Recommended for the Distinguished Service Order. This Officer was in Command of the advanced en n.C's. On his	
			as follows:-	
			FRESNOY 16th August 1917: way there he continued the mopping up of an intermediate position (IBERNIA), capturing	

A6945 Wt. W14422/M1160 350,000 12/16 D. D. & L. Forms/C/2118/14

Army Form C. 2118.

WAR DIARY
or
INTELLIGENCE SUMMARY.

(Erase heading not required.)

7th R.Inniskilling Fusrs.   Page 145.

Place	Date	Hour	Summary of Events and Information	Remarks and references to Appendices
			with the help of the small party forming advanced on M.G's. & M/G's and some 50 prisoners, who had been overlooked by the party specially detailed for this purpose. He then proceeded to the advance on M.G's (DELVA FARM). On the battalion being forced back from the position running through Hill 37 and in front of DELVA FARM on which it was consolidating itself, as a result of both its flanks being exposed and the advance of the enemy who threatened to encircle them, he by his coolness, courage and good leadership was responsible for its orderly retirement as far as a line running through INFRULA. Practically all the Officers were killed, wounded or missing, and the Casualties amongst the O.R's by this time were about 60 %. He himself was wounded. By his resolute action, the advance of the enemy in their Counter-attack was delayed and finally stopped, and consequently the troops in rear were given time to take up covering defensive positions.	
			2nd Lieut Francis Desmond MURPHY. Recommended for the Military Cross as follows:—	
			YPRES, 16th August 1917: For conspicuous gallantry and able leadership. This officer distinguished himself in the Battle of WYTSCHAETE on the 7.6.17, and again in the fighting of the 16.8.17 by his personal example assisted materially in the advance to	

Army Form C. 2118.

WAR DIARY
or
INTELLIGENCE SUMMARY.

(Erase heading not required.) 7th R.Inniskilling Fusrs. Page 146.

Place	Date	Hour	Summary of Events and Information	Remarks and references to Appendices
			the final objective of the battalion. Later when the battalion was forced to retire owing to adverse circumstances, although wounded in several places, he refused to leave the battalion: the majority of officers of which had already become Casualties, and by his pluck and coolness materially assisted in re-organising and holding the line. He has since been evacuated and has to undergo an operation to remove the fragments of shell etc which had lodged in him.	
			23618 Corporal Frank SMITH. Recommended for the Distinguished Conduct Medal as follows:- YPRES, 16th August 1917. This N.C.O. showed conspicuous gallantry of a very high order, which combined with his personality enabled him at a critical moment, when men were falling back to rally them and lead them forward again. These men were of all ranks and from various units. Moreover generally throughout the day he was ceaseless and untiring in carrying out his own special duties and even found time to help others in theirs.	
			The causes of the failure in this attack would appear to have been amongst other points:-	

Army Form C. 2118.

WAR DIARY
or
INTELLIGENCE SUMMARY.
(Erase heading not required.) 7th R. Inniskilling Fusrs. Page 147.

Instructions regarding War Diaries and Intelligence Summaries are contained in F. S. Regs., Part II. and the Staff Manual respectively. Title pages will be prepared in manuscript.

Place	Date	Hour	Summary of Events and Information	Remarks and references to Appendices
O.B. front line.	16/17.		1. Insufficient preparation due to the bad weather. 2. " depth in the attack. A brigade in the O.B. & O.G. lines would certainly have turned defeat into victory; a battalion even would probably have turned the scale. 3. Bad communications to the rear, which was only maintained by Runner. 4. Troops on either flank not moving close enough up to the barrage, thus giving the Germans time to get their M/G's in action. 5. Unsatisfactory "Mopping up". 6. Want of depth in the artillery barrage. 7. Lack of powers of leadership on the part of N.C.O's, when their Officers had fallen. The battalion moved back into the old British front line immediately S of the YPRES -ZONNEBEKE Road arriving there about 11.50 p.m. Strength 7 Officers and 114 O.R's. Maj Kerr, M.C. had meanwhile come up to the Bde Office temporarily to assist the acting Staff Captain.	
	17	8-30 p.m.	The battalion moved to BIVOUAC Camp about ¾ mile S. E of VLAMERTINGHE, which they had previously occupied as a battalion from the 1.8.17; this time the whole Brigade, including Brigade H.Q's,	

Army Form C. 2118.

WAR DIARY
or
INTELLIGENCE SUMMARY.
(Erase heading not required.)

7th R.Inniskilling Fusrs.   Page 148.

Instructions regarding War Diaries and Intelligence Summaries are contained in F. S. Regs., Part II. and the Staff Manual respectively. Title pages will be prepared in manuscript.

Place	Date	Hour	Summary of Events and Information	Remarks and references to Appendices
	18		H/Q Coy and L.M.G. were encamped there. A/Lieut H.P.McKenna replaced Maj Kerr, who returned to Echelon "B" at the brigade.	
			Lt Col H.B.Young, D.S.O. took over temporary Command of the 49th Infy Brigade and 2nd Lieut A.H.H.Armstrong that of the Battalion.	
			The Battalion embussed at VLAMERTINGHE together with the remainder of the Brigade and moved to WARCO "C" area when it was rejoined by its Echelon "B", including Major Kerr,M.C. Captain, Stainforth,M.C. 2nd Lieut G.J.Metcalfe, A/Lieut H.F.Reid,Transport Officer and Lieut & Qr Mr W.Reid.	
			Maj R.G.Kerr,M.C. took over Command of the Battalion from 2nd Lieut A.H.H.Armstrong. Battalion remained in their billets and camp.GODEWAERSWELDE. H.Q's, A & B Coy being in billets; C & D Coys and the Transport in Tents.	
	19		In same billets and camp.	
			15 new L/G's complete with drums received.	
	20		Orders received re the move of the Battalion to the 3rd Army.	
	21		Battalion moved off via CASSEL to BAVINCHOVE about 6 p.m. and lay out in a field,pending entraining. Before entraining the Battalion had an issue of rum and some tea.	

WAR DIARY
or
INTELLIGENCE SUMMARY.

(Erase heading not required.)   7th R.Inniskilling Fus.   Page 149.

Army Form C. 2118.

Place	Date	Hour	Summary of Events and Information	Remarks and references to Appendices
	22		The battalion commenced to entrain at 3-20 a.m. The transport having already been entrained.	
			The train moved out at 4-50 a.m. and arrived at MIRAMONT at 12-50 p.m. On arrival it	
			immediately moved off to ACHIET – LE – PETIT, about 2 miles N where it moved into shelters.	
			Battn R.O. 1236.d/21.8.17. Special order: Officers and men of the fighting "seventh"	
			Inniskillings. The more one learns of the battle of the 16th Augt at YPRES, when you advanced	
			fearlessly against strong opposition as only true "Inniskillings" can and captured all your	
			objects including hill 37,IBERNIA FARM,BEUK FARM right up to the LANGEMARCK – GHELUVELT line	
			and then hung on there until forced back by overwhelming numbers,both your flanks having long	
			since been exposed,the more pride one should feel in belonging to such a body of men.	
			You have nobly upheld the honour and traditions of your battalion and parent regiment and by	
			your courage and devotion to duty won fresh laurels for them.	
			Our casualties were very severe,out of 20 Officers and 472 men,who went into action,only 7	
			Officers and 114 O.R's came out with the battalion. All ranks must now endeavour to reform	
			and organise the battalion so that we shall be ready again when called upon.	
			(Sd) A.W.Young, A/Brig Gen. 49th Infy Bde.	
ACHIET-LE-PETIT.	23		The 8th Battn R.Innis Fus was amalgamated with the battalion.	

WAR DIARY
or
INTELLIGENCE SUMMARY.
(Erase heading not required.)

7th R.Inniskilling Fusrs. Page 150.

Army Form C. 2118.

Place	Date	Hour	Summary of Events and Information	Remarks and references to Appendices
	23		The following officers joined the battalion:	
			Major &a/Lt Col A.J.MAHKEY,M.C. (supernumerary,attached.); Captn W.E.H.MUIR,M.C. (supernumerary,attached.); Lieut & Q.M.J.SEARLE (Supernumerary,attached.); Captn A.A.GREEN,M.C.; Captn F.W.MARTIN; Lieut & a/Captn H.J.GROOMBRIDGE; Lieut C.J.COGGINS; Lieut C.H.QUIN; Lieut W.F.ELLIS,M.C. (On leave); 2nd Lieut A.H.HOPKINS (On leave).	
			On R.O. I277. d/25.8.17. COMMAND BATTN: Lt Col R.H.Young, D.S.O. reassumed Command of the battn on return of Brig Gen Leveson-Gower, with effect from 23.8.17.	
			On R.O. I240.d/23.8.17.DESIGNATION OF THE BATTN: In future the battalion will be known as the 7/8th Royal Inniskilling Fusiliers.	
			On R.O. I239. d/23.8.17. SPECIAL ORDER: Officers and other ranks of the old 7th and 8th battns of the Royal Inniskilling Fusiliers are from this date amalgamated as one battalion. Both battalions as such they must continue to accrue fresh honours for their parent regiment. Both battalions have records of which any battalion in the British army would be proud to possess. Let it now be the aim of all to win a name for the combined battns which will if possible,even surpass the record of either.	

Army Form C. 2118.

WAR DIARY
or
INTELLIGENCE SUMMARY.

(Erase heading not required.)

7th R.Inniskilling Fusrs.　Page 151.

Instructions regarding War Diaries and Intelligence Summaries are contained in F. S. Regs., Part II. and the Staff Manual respectively. Title pages will be prepared in manuscript.

Place	Date	Hour	Summary of Events and Information	Remarks and references to Appendices
			Bn R.O. 1241.d/23.8.17: OFFICERS.DISTRIBUTION OF:	
			C.O. Lt Col H.M.YOUNG, D.S.O.	
			Senior Major. Major R.G.KERR, M.C.	
			Adjutant. Captain A.C.TAGGART. C Coy.	
			Asst " Lieut C.J.COGGINS. A "	
			Signalling Officer. 2/Lieut H.P.H.Montgomery. B "	
			Intelligence " " A.H.ROBBINS. C "	
			Transport " A/Lieut A.F.REID. A "	
			Asst " " Lieut C.H.QUIN. D "	
			Quartermaster. " W.REID.	
			Medical Officer. Captain G.O.F.ALLEY, M.C.	
			"D" COMPANY.	
			"A" COMPANY.	
			Captn F.W.MARTIN. Captn H.A.GREEN,M.C.	
			Lieut W.F.ELLIS. (Instr 16th I.B.D.)	
			2nd " J.F.O'BRIEN. Lieut A.E.C.TRIMBLE.	
			" " H.LILLEY. a/" H.P.McKENNA. attchd brigade.	
			2/" H.V.LOWRY.	

Army Form C. 2118.

WAR DIARY
or
INTELLIGENCE SUMMARY.

(Erase heading not required.) 7th R.Inniskilling Fusrs. Page 152.

Instructions regarding War Diaries and Intelligence Summaries are contained in F. S. Regs., Part II. and the Staff Manual respectively. Title pages will be prepared in manuscript.

Place	Date	Hour	Summary of Events and Information	Remarks and references to Appendices
			"C" COMPANY:	
			Lieut & A/Captn A.N.SEWARD.	
			2nd Lieut A.H.H.ARMSTRONG.	
			" " C.W.FAWKES.	
			" " F.D.MORPHY.	
			" " R.A.B.LINDOP.	
			"D" COMPANY:	
			Captn C.H.STAINFORTH, M.C.	
			Lieut & A/Captn H.G.GROOMBRIDGE.	
			2nd Lieut C.J.METCALFE.	
			" " R.A.B.LINDOP.	
			" " Captn W.E.H.MUIR, M.C.	
			SUPERNUMERARY:	
			Major & A/Lt Col A.J.WALKEY, M.C.	
			Lieut & Qr Mr G.SEARLE, M.C.	
			Bn H.Q. 1842.d./23.8.17. W.O's.POSTING OF:	
			R.S.M. 5408 C.S.M. & A/R.S.M. W.THOMPSON. D Coy.	
			R.Q.M.S. 15105 R.Q.M.S R.WILSON. C	
			H.Q. COMPANY: A/C.S.M. & A/C.Q.M.S.- 13598 Sgt & A/C.S.M. T.CUNNINGHAM	
			"A" COMPANY:	
			29115 C.S.M. E.E.KNIGG.	
			13853 C.Q.M.S. R.RIDDELL.	
			"B" COMPANY:	
			19652 A/C.S.M. B.MURREDD.	
			24750 C.Q.M.S. H.BARLOW.	

Army Form C. 2118.

WAR DIARY
or
INTELLIGENCE SUMMARY.

(Erase heading not required.)   7th R.Inniskilling Fusrs.   Page 153.

Place	Date	Hour	Summary of Events and Information	Remarks and references to Appendices
			"B" COMPANY:	
			13452 C.S.M. J.KERDY	
			13068 C.Q.M.S. J.GILCHRIST	
			"D" COMPANY:	
			8418 C.S.M. C.McDONNELL	
			18786 C.Q.M.S. J.LOUDEN	
			13060 C.Q.M.S. C.WILSON	
			SUPERNUMERARY:	
			12991 R.S.M.S. R.BOAL. D. Coy. 18177 C.S.M. D.MERNOR. C. Coy.	
			13023 C.S.M. M.COLGAN. A " 20099 C.S.M. J.GOULDEN. B "
			18140 C.Q.M.S. C.A.SHAW. C " 10030 C.Q.M.S. M.KILLEN. A "
			18090 C.Q.M.S. J.JAMES. B "	
			Orders for their disposal will be issued later, meanwhile with the exception noted below	
			they will remain attached to their Coys as shewn above.	
			R.Q.M.S. BOAL will remain attached to the Q.M. Dept.	
	24		A/Lieut A.F.McKenna returned to duty with the Battalion from the Brigade on return of the	
			Staff Captain.	
	25		2nd Lieut F.D.MORPHY admitted to Hospital as a result of wounds received in action on the	
			16.8.17.	

Army Form C. 2118.

WAR DIARY
or
INTELLIGENCE SUMMARY.

(Erase heading not required.)

7th R.Inniskilling Fusrs. 154.

Instructions regarding War Diaries and Intelligence Summaries are contained in F. S. Regs., Part II. and the Staff Manual respectively. Title pages will be prepared in manuscript.

Place	Date	Hour	Summary of Events and Information	Remarks and references to Appendices
ACHIET-LE-PETIT.	28.		Captn H.J.IRELAND, and 2nd Lieut J.F.O'BRIEN, leave to England 26.8.17 – 5.9.17. Notified that 2nd Lieut C.CLARKE relinquishes his Commission on account of ill health, no date given. Auth 5507/2. M.S.K 504. G/8.8.17. He was wounded on the 14.6.16.	
BRVILLERS.	28.		The Division relieved the 51st Div less its artillery in the line-approximately BULLECOURT - FONTAINE les CROISILLES; the Brigade moving into Divisional Reserve, the Battalion moving into a HIPPED BOW Camp at BRVILLERS. Officers visited the same afternoon the left Bde Hdqrs and its support & reserve Battalions and also the Right Brigade. Heavy showers all day.	
	29.		The C.O. & 2/Lt Coggins A/Adjt visited Left Bde H.Qds and the reserve and support Battalions. Heavy showers all day. Lieut & A/Captn W.J.Groombridge ordered by the Brigade S.C.O./951. d/29.8.17 to report immediately to the 7/8 R.Ir Fus for duty, also warned at same time that Lieut C.J.Coggins would be required to report there also in a few days for duty.	
"	30.		Heavy showers all day.	
"	"		Still in Divisional Reserve.	

Army Form C. 2118.

WAR DIARY
or
INTELLIGENCE SUMMARY.

(Erase heading not required.) 7/6 R Innis' Fusiliers Page 155

Place	Date	Hour	Summary of Events and Information	Remarks and references to Appendices
ERVILLERS	Aug 31		Lieut C.J. Coggins arrived to report to the 7/6 R. Ir. Fus. 9 or duty with effect from the 27/8/17, authoree #1502 dd 30/8/17. Slept in camp overnight in the weather. Lines and lighter showers of rain.	
No 5 Camp.			Fighting strength returns shows 31 Officers and 1245 O.R's. in the strength of 7th Battalion. The airtight return strength returns 12 Officers and 665 O.R.S. This large difference accounted for by the fact that a 151 O.R's from the 8 = R Innis Fus is on not yet joined the period to comparison. The Camp (N.5) renamed ENNISKILLEN Camp.	
			31/8/17.	
				A.H. Gurney Lt.Col. 7/6 5 R Innis Killing Fus ?

www.ingramcontent.com/pod-product-compliance
Lightning Source LLC
Chambersburg PA
CBHW051526190426
43193CB00045BA/2115